# FIRE IN THE BELLY

### HOW PURDY CRAWFORD RESCUED CANADA
### AND CHANGED THE WAY WE DO BUSINESS

## Gordon Pitts

## NIMBUS
### PUBLISHING

Nimbus Publishing Limited
3731 Mackintosh St, Halifax, NS B3K 5A5
(902) 455-4286 nimbus.ca

Printed and bound in Canada

NB1165

Cover photo: Dean Palmer
Design: Peggy Issenman, Peggy & Co. Design

Library and Archives Canada Cataloguing in Publication

Pitts, Gordon, author
Fire in the belly : how Purdy Crawford rescued Canada and changed the way
we do business / Gordon Pitts.
    Includes bibliographical references.
    Issued in print and electronic formats.
    ISBN 978-1-77108-178-8 (bound).–ISBN 978-1-77108-179-5 (html).
    –ISBN 978-1-77108-222-8 (mobi)
1. Crawford, Purdy. 2. Mentoring in business–Canada. 3. Leadership–Canada.
4. Lawyers–Canada–Biography.
I. Title.

KE416.C73P58 2014        340.092        C2014-903175-0
KF345.Z9P58 2014                         C2014-903176-9

Canada Council  Conseil des arts
for the Arts    du Canada

FILM & CREATIVE INDUSTRIES
NOVA SCOTIA

Nimbus Publishing acknowledges the financial support for its publishing
activities from the Government of Canada through the Canada Book Fund
(CBF) and the Canada Council for the Arts, and from the Province of Nova
Scotia through Film & Creative Industries Nova Scotia. We are pleased to work
in partnership with Film & Creative Industries Nova Scotia to develop and
promote our creative industries for the benefit of all Nova Scotians.

# CONTENTS

# Foreword

This book is a biography of Purdy Crawford, esteemed lawyer and business executive, and the man who led "the largest and by far the most complex restructuring in Canada's history," according to *American Lawyer* magazine: the 2008 rescue of the $35 billion market in non-bank asset-backed commercial paper. It is a book about an exceptional man who has made an invaluable contribution to law and business in Canada.

But my foreword is a more personal take. Purdy Crawford is my friend—first, a neighbour whom I met in 1968 when my family moved to Toronto from Winnipeg. My wife was not a happy camper about the move because she frequently had been told that Toronto was a cold, unfriendly place. We quickly found the opposite was true because we met the Crawfords, a transplanted couple from Nova Scotia, and their five children (a sixth would be born a few years later). Our wives and school-age children soon became close, and we integrated into the incredibly friendly and welcoming North Toronto neighbourhood almost before the moving trucks had left.

While our kids played road hockey right in front of the Crawfords' house, I met Purdy across the back fence and soon discovered we had a great deal in common. We were both raised in small villages (Purdy's in Nova Scotia, mine in rural Saskatchewan); attended small liberal arts universities; enjoyed demanding professional lives; and were very much involved with our growing and active families. Perhaps most satisfying, in the context of our friendship, was the discovery that we both loved the written word.

And so we became friends, with our friendship often cemented over a Friday night Scotch at his home and with enthusiastic arguments, which today his children describe as loud. Purdy was a nonpartisan supporter of governments—including Pierre Trudeau's, which I couldn't abide as a partisan Prairie Tory. And, unlike Purdy, I couldn't sing, which he does beautifully and enthusiastically, or play golf, which he loved. Purdy also played college sports, including football and hockey. According to his Harvard Law School contemporary, former finance minister Donald Macdonald, "he was without any shadow of a doubt the best player on the ice and the smoothest skating defenceman you ever saw."

In 1985, Purdy and his wife Bea left Toronto for Montreal, where he became CEO of Imasco, and there was great sadness in the neighbourhood—the Crawford Christmas party and carol sing had been a major event each year. But life moved on and Purdy moved with it, as he had been doing since he left Five Islands, Nova Scotia, for Mount Allison University at age seventeen, then on to Dalhousie Law School, and from there to Harvard for a post-graduate degree. He eventually ended up at Osler, a prestigious Toronto law firm, and went on to a lifetime of achievements of which most people only dream. But in pursuing his own great career, Purdy has always taken time to inspire others to pursue excellence. He has always focused on the big picture and, although a true rainmaker, he has been humane and compassionate in dealing with people. In this way, he became a gravitational force: like the Bay of Fundy tide, so fundamental to the Glooscap Trail that remains a part of his life, Purdy Crawford raises all boats, not just his own.

Who knows what makes a friend? The best description I ever read was in a poem by Emily Dickinson: "The soul selects her own society," she writes, then "shuts the door/To her divine majority/ Intrude no more." In truth, I don't know what Purdy has gained from our friendship, but I do know what I have gained from his. He demonstrated the importance of listening, rather than talking. He surprised me when he always spoke highly of other legal firms—I picked up the practice and emulated him. He knew how to work a room, and I tried to follow his example. And he loved to stir the pot, not to be ornery, but to change an insipid conversation into an inspired one.

I like the description of friendship by an American writer: "A friend is one who knows you and likes you just the same." Whatever the reason, knowing Purdy Crawford has been a wonderful life experience that permits me to salute my former neighbour and constant friend and to reflect on the value of that friendship. It is a friendship that endures, even with Purdy's passing in August 2014.

*Joe Martin is the director of Canadian business history and executive in residence at the Rotman School of Management, University of Toronto.*

Introduction

# THE BOY FROM FIVE ISLANDS

I t is an afternoon in mid-August 2007, and Purdy Crawford, the arthritic but energetic Bay Street lawyer, has returned to Toronto from a carefree summer in his boyhood town of Five Islands, Nova Scotia. Tanned after days in the sun, memories still fresh of clam dinners and lively conversation in his family's century-old farmhouse, he is sitting in the downtown Toronto office of Osler, Hoskin & Harcourt, the blue-chip law firm that has been his base—and his laboratory—for some of the most transformative change in Canadian business.

This is the place from which he masterminded a revolution in Canadian law, set the standard for corporate governance, wrote the rules for capital markets, saved and nurtured a university, and mentored the country's business elite. At seventy-five, he is semi-retired and pulling back a bit, enjoying a life that takes him from his Five Islands retreat to city and country homes in Toronto and a winter place in Florida—and gives him time to dote on his fifteen (soon to reach seventeen) grandchildren.

His telephone buzzes, and on the line is Henri-Paul Rousseau, head of the powerful Caisse de dépôt et placement du Québec, Canada's largest pension fund manager. There is urgency in his voice. Rousseau wants Purdy to rescue him, his pension fund, and Canadian financial markets from a hundred-car pileup of a crisis.

As a senior corporate lawyer and director, deeply involved in the financial world and widely read, Crawford knows that world is teetering on calamity. The US housing market is rife with tainted, sub-prime mortgages and, after a wave of mad speculation, the US property vortex is spiralling downward. The sub-prime mortgages are the shaky foundation of a flimsy edifice of derivatives and structured products that financiers have devised to earn huge fees, oblivious to the risk they pose to the global economy. Now, the great fear is that bundles of investments sold to Canadians contain these dubious mortgages, and tremors of fear have spread to a little-known corner of the Canadian financial system: the arcane, opaque market in third-party, asset-backed commercial paper (ABCP). The market has scarily frozen, stranding $35 billion of supposedly safe assets held by pension funds, companies, and almost two thousand individual investors who have their retirement savings, their children's tuition, and their house deposits tied up in these vehicles.

And no one is more heavily invested than Rousseau, a bristly bear of a man with a PhD in economics from the University of Western Ontario and a larger-than-life personality. The Caisse helped create this market and now holds $13.2 billion worth of the imperilled paper. As he huddles with other Quebec institutions and confers with a worried federal finance department and the Bank of Canada, Rousseau concludes there is one man with the network, the work ethic, the prestige, to save the situation. Would Purdy take on what has become known as the ABCP crisis? It is a Churchillian moment— the chance to do something truly history making in the autumn of his career.

The job is a monster, far overshadowing what Crawford has done before. And yet he has never shrunk from challenges since leaving Five Islands for the first time at age seventeen and travelling a hundred kilometres down the road to Sackville, New Brunswick, and Mount Allison University. That road has extended to Boston, Montreal, and

Toronto, but in many ways he is still that boy with the wavy hair and unruly cowlick that dangles down over his forehead.

There is something preternaturally youthful in the easy grin, the sparkling eyes, the aw-shucks rural talk—but there is also the wear and tear of decades of hard work, fine dining, and hit-and-miss exercise. A fine athlete as a youth, a cyclist and golfer in his prime, he has been carrying a fair bit of weight and now sports a round belly that, as his friend Frank McKenna says, gives the impression of "a smiling Buddha." The arthritic feet, the knee replacements, and the chronic asthma have slowed but not stopped him.

He seems uncharismatic and is no great orator—no stirring Purdy quotes remain in the memory. He is the antithesis of the table-pounding, Type A personality CEO that the business press likes to write about. Margaret McCain, his friend for six decades, says the roughest words she has heard attributed to him, reported after a board meeting of her family's company, Maple Leaf Foods, were: "It sounds to me like the goddamn turkeys are running the farm."

But then you hear people talk of Crawford's electric impact one-on-one or in small groups—calling him a "natural leader," "magnetic," "charming." His attraction, then, lies in the disarming smile, the small touches, the ability to nudge a conversation, to reach a vote, and to touch people's lives with a gentle word, a note, a phone call, or an article or book that he kindly passes on, suggesting "here is something you might consider." As a boy, he wanted to grow up to be a sawmill virtuoso, shaping well-cut boards; instead, he crafts leaders and shapes Canadian boardrooms as a business virtuoso. The people who run Canada are Purdy's people, the people he has mentored.

One of them, CBC news anchor Peter Mansbridge, says the Crawford style of persuasion is subtle. "It's not like, if you say no, you are going to find the horse's head in your bed the next morning. It's just that you have such enormous respect for him, that he has shown he cares about you in the most fundamental way—in trying to make you a better person and better in your professional life." For Purdy, that was always the essence of mentoring—taking an interest in people, often younger but also his peers, and wanting to make them better. He was mentored himself—by senior lawyers, sage CEOs, family, and friends—before becoming the go-to mentor in Canadian business and public life.

And it's not as though Peter Mansbridge and the others Purdy has mentored call him every day for nuggets of advice. He and Mansbridge meet from time to time and talk about the newsman's future. Occasionally, Purdy requests a favour: would Mansbridge talk to a group? At his most daring, he recruited the CBC anchor to become chancellor of Purdy's beloved Mount Allison University. "You are not going to say no to Purdy Crawford," Mansbridge says firmly.

Through this quiet, patient outreach, he has, over the past sixty years, emerged as Canada's most influential business leader—not the richest, the loudest, or most headline-grabbing, but the most influential. David Thomson and Galen Weston I and II are incredibly wealthy family scions; the TV Dragons are daredevil entrepreneurs; Frank Stronach has created untold value in auto parts; but Purdy Crawford has shaped how Canadians do business, how they buy stocks and bonds, how women advance, how people lead, how corporate governance functions, how public institutions raise money—and how leaders mentor new leaders. He has played an important role in transforming Canadian business from the old world of family dynasties, quiet money, and old school ties to an era of professionalism, meritocracy, highly scrutinized governance, and the public corporation. He is a catalyst for modernization in universities, law firms, and businesses. He has never gone to the barricades; instead, he has worked inside the system, pushing for change with respect, consensus, and a nudge here and there. But make no mistake: he has been a game-changer.

And now, with Rousseau's call, he is being asked to take on a crisis that, if he fails, could bring down the Canadian financial system.

He assesses the resources at his disposal. Purdy's people are the leaders of Canada. In Atlantic Canada are the prominent families he has counselled—the McCains, the Braggs, the Sobeys; in universities are the people, such as University of Waterloo president (and future governor general) David Johnston, whose careers he has advanced. Then there is Mount Allison, the model of the successful small university that he helped to mould and where the Crawford legacy of financial security and league-leading academic quality continues.

On Bay Street, Osler, Hoskin & Harcourt is his great creation, one of the first major law firms built on the principle of merit, not bloodlines. It now ranks among the Seven Sisters, the popular label for the firms that dominate Canadian corporate law. Other firms have emulated Purdy's template for building an upper-tier practice, and he has a deep fan base of lawyers who work in hedge funds, investment firms, and corporate legal departments.

His handiwork is evident in the leadership of companies such as Canadian National Railway and Shoppers Drug Mart. And nowhere is he more influential than at the Toronto-Dominion Bank, Canada's second-largest financial institution. It might even be called Purdy's Bank, although he never worked there and sat on its board for just the blink of an eye. His influence lies in the people he has backed. His protegé Ed Clark is the CEO, his friend Frank McKenna is the bank's roving ambassador, and a core of the bank's senior officers hails from the 1980s and 1990s when Purdy helped lay its modern foundations in his oversight role at Canada Trust, the acquisition that transformed TD. Purdy's people also work in the major regulatory bodies for capital markets—from the Ontario Securities Commission to the principal regulator of the investment industry—and in the pension funds that now call the shots on the street. And many of them are women—Purdy was gender blind before it was fashionable.

"He is a like a puppeteer," McKenna says, describing his friend's ability to pull strings to put the right people in the right places.

And he is not a front-runner, McKenna avers. In his mentoring, "he's overweighted in people who aren't successful yet." Purdy believes in underdogs and their potential to become top dogs. After all, he was one himself, having started life in a small village and received his first education in a two-room schoolhouse. Encouraged by his father, a coal miner, and his mother, a force of nature, he was the offspring of a May-December marriage that produced just one shining, golden boy. He is a Canadian Horatio Alger hero, a product of pluck and luck.

"He proves you don't have to come from blueblood lineage to succeed," says Susan Wolburgh Jenah, then Canada's top investment industry regulator and one of the many female beneficiaries of the Purdy school of mentoring. "He embraced emotional intelligence before it was fashionable, and he embraced diversity—the idea that everyone should have a shot. He took the time and effort to promote people when he saw passion." And passion, Wolburgh Jenah says, is the key differentiator for Purdy. Intelligence is essential, but the rare, critical ingredient is "fire in the belly."

His other staple is taking on big, tough jobs in public life. He has been doing it since he was a young lawyer, but he is now seventy-five and does not need this assignment to solve the ABCP crisis. He is wealthy and successful far beyond the dreams of the boy who first left home in Five Islands in the late 1940s. But he loves the business game, he loves public service, and he loves the idea of diving once more into a game-saving project. Besides, he figures, he can clean up this mess in a few months. He has numerous ailments but feels well enough for one more game. "He is like an old Labrador who sees the gun and has to struggle to his feet to get the bird," says Brian Levitt, his old friend, protegé, and soon-to-be chairman of the TD Bank.

It is as if Crawford's whole life and career were a preparation for this moment. It brings together the arsenal of skills and networks—his negotiating savvy, his patience and persistence, his ties with elites from Vancouver to St. John's, and his ability to converse with and understand anyone. He often has had to find common ground with difficult people in difficult situations. He says "they are good people," which means "they may be ornery, they may be impossible, but I can see the good in them, and I can work with them." It is a philosophy that has its roots in a different time and place.

Chapter One

# BUCKING THE WIND

Purdy Crawford grew up in the land of the great god-man Glooscap, who, according to Mi'kmaq legend, was locked in fierce battle with his constant enemy, the beaver. In his rage, Glooscap threw a fusillade of mud, stone, and sand in the direction of the pesky varmint. The debris flew past the beaver and scattered across Minas Basin, in the northeast corner of the Bay of Fundy, creating five islands, each a distinctive shape and size. Over the years, they attracted colourful names: Moose, Diamond, Egg, and Pinnacle (the fifth is the more prosaic Long). Ever since the age of Glooscap, the islands have been haunted places of mystery and myth. On Moose Island, in the 1840s, a Scotsman named John Ruff waged an abusive reign of terror against his family until he died in a mysterious accident. Two of his sons were accused of killing the old man but were acquitted of the crime—and yet the question lingers: how did the old tyrant die? John Ruff's ghost is said to wander across Moose Island, often gazing across to the craggy mainland point known as Old Wife Rock. So far, he has provided no clue as to his cause of death.

At low tide, you can walk from the islands to the shore and then along stretches of beach, from which the land rises up to Highway 2, the road between Truro and Parrsboro, to a little community known, naturally enough, as Five Islands. There, in a sturdy white-frame house is where a quieter, less violent, but no less legendary figure, Purdy Crawford, was born in the fall of 1931. Across the road from the house is the two-room schoolhouse where he got his early education and a ball field where he learned to play a slick second base—although he couldn't quite solve the southpaw offerings of another local legend, an ace pitcher known as Mountain Boy.

Growing up, Crawford's view from that white-frame house out to the mysterious islands inspired a yearning, a sense that there were worlds to conquer out there beyond the village, beyond Minas Basin. He embarked on a voyage that took him to Sackville, Halifax, Boston, and ultimately to the office canyons of Montreal and Toronto where he became the most distinguished corporate lawyer and business leader of his time.

But he never really left Five Islands, either physically—he would return each summer—or in the values hard earned by digging for clams, stacking lumber in his half-brothers' sawmill, and absorbing the life lessons of a battered coal-mining father and a fiercely ambitious survivor of a mother. He learned tolerance and respect, patience and persistence, the idea that the world does not hand you a living, that you have to work hard for everything you get. You don't let the little things distract you, but you see the big goal off on the horizon—beyond Five Islands, beyond Nova Scotia. You never forget the people who helped you on the voyage, and you extend a hand to those who come after you.

His father Frank grew up directly north of Five Islands, in Wallace, Nova Scotia, up along the Northumberland Strait across from Charlottetown. Frank lived with his mother and stepfather, but there was a row with his stepfather, and he was thrown out of the house at age fourteen and went to work in the coal mines of Springhill, a town whose name became synonymous with tragic mining accidents. He won attention from his employers, later going to mining school and rising to "overman"—basically an underground foreman—in the

No. 2 Springhill mine. He was a strong man who could lift big rocks and commanded respect from workers and managers alike. During strikes, when miners blocked entrance to the colliery, family legend says Frank was the only manager allowed to enter without resistance. He was often summoned by the town police to help break up bar fights in the mining town.

Frank managed to be spared the big accidents that gave Springhill its chilling notoriety—he was off work during the explosion that, in 1891, killed 125 miners, and was retired by the time of the 1956 blast that took 39 lives and the 1958 mine collapse that claimed 74 more. The disasters have overshadowed even the fame of Springhill's most famous offspring, singer Anne Murray. Yet, in a region that has known more than its share of grief, Frank could not dodge death forever. He married, raised a family of two sons and a daughter, but lost a son to rheumatic fever and then, in the aftermath of the First World War, saw his family devastated by the Spanish flu epidemic. His wife Mary took sick, but as she seemed to improve, Frank went back to work. Later that day, someone called down the mine shaft that "Frank's wife has died." There was another Frank working in the mine that day, and there was a moment of cruel confusion. But Frank Crawford soon realized it was his Mary who had perished. His remaining son, two-year-old Freddy, was also weak from the flu, and that night, as Frank tried to comfort his family, Freddy died in his arms, leaving him and daughter Vi alone in the world.

In his late fifties, he happened to meet Grace MacAloney, a divorced woman from Five Islands in her late twenties with two children of her own. Grace was a feisty survivor: at birth, she was so tiny that her head could fit in a tea cup. Her mother Eliza was diagnosed with terminal breast cancer during the pregnancy, and her father, unable to cope, took off, leaving Grace to be raised, lovingly, by an uncle and aunt. As a young woman, Grace saw her first husband walk away, leaving her to raise two boys by herself. Then she met Frank Crawford and, about 1930, they married and set up house in Grace's hometown of Five Islands. Grace's two boys and Frank's daughter were soon joined, in a kind of second-chance miracle, by a child of the couple's own: Harold Purdy Crawford, born November 7, 1931, who grew up as the apple of his parents' eye.

Purdy is a family name. Purdys lived in Westchester County, north of New York City, and fought on both sides during the American Revolution. After the conflict, one of the big brood, Gabriel Purdy, ended up in Nova Scotia. In time, the Purdys married into the Crawfords, an old family from the British Isles. Purdy doesn't know why he got his name, but there was a lot of mixing and matching of old family names—in fact, Purdy Crawford has a cousin named Crawford Purdy.

After years of working underground, Frank, worn out and suffering from diabetes and various mining injuries, retired to Five Islands. He enjoyed another quarter-century watching his family grow up. For Purdy, it was an odd sensation knowing that, by the time he was born, he had lost two half-brothers to illness and had a half-sister who was older than his mother and a full generation older than he. And he had two teenaged half-brothers, Hal and James, who loved him dearly and took him under their wings. Everyone, it seems, loved Purdy. As a little boy, he could expect that, every weekend, his dad would buy him oranges, which were not to be shared. When Purdy was old enough to drive, one or the other of his brothers would give up his car every other weekend so that Purdy would not be left high and dry to court and play ball.

Clearly, this Golden Boy had every reason to grow up spoiled, but that is not anyone's recollection of Purdy. Right from the start, there was this sensitivity about people and their feelings. As a kid, walking along the road one day with a friend and another neighbour, he made an offhand remark about the friend's mother stepping out in an extramarital affair. The careless comment cost him the boy's friendship for a while—they repaired their relationship, but it was never the same. And seventy years later, it haunted him as one of his great regrets. He would never again be so thoughtless in his talk.

He was a strong athlete—he played hockey and baseball—and a good student, sailing through grades 1 to 10 in the two-room schoolhouse at Five Islands. He actually took grades 7 and 8 in one year, a common practice for precocious youngsters in small rural schools. He took grades 11 and 12 at the four-room schoolhouse in Bass River, about fifteen miles east of Five Islands. In those days, there was no easy daily commuting, so Purdy boarded with a family in Bass River and came home on weekends, often hitchhiking down the Truro–Parrsboro road on Friday afternoons.

Bass River is a pretty little place, a sharp corner on the ruggedly wooded highway, but the bucolic setting masked hard, grinding poverty despite the presence of a furniture factory that turned out sturdy chairs. There, Purdy excelled in school, and he also got to know Beatrice Corbett, a bright teenaged girl who was two years his junior. There was chemistry between the two from the beginning, Bea says. She had always known of Purdy Crawford's existence. During the summer, she would visit her grandparents in Five Islands, where the Corbetts were among the earliest settlers—an ancestor had been given a land grant there after fighting with Wolfe at Quebec. "However, it wasn't until high school that I started to notice this handsome blond curly headed guy...and soon we were dating and he became the love of my life."

If Purdy's background was plain, Bea's upbringing was grim. "We were as poor as hedgehogs, but everybody in that community was real poor," she says. "It was a way of life—no inside plumbing, cold houses, and my father struggled to make enough. I thought that was somewhat normal." Purdy and Bea's kids were told that, in winter, it was so cold in the Corbett home that the pee in the chamber pot would freeze.

Bea's mother Helene was afflicted with multiple sclerosis, but she was a clever woman who always had a venture going to make money. She had to, because her husband Wilfred perpetually struggled to make ends meet. She sold homemade candy in Bass River; then, during the Second World War, after Wilfred moved the family to Pictou, Nova Scotia, so he could work in the bustling wartime shipyard, Helene went door-to-door selling lingerie from a Quebec catalogue—"in spite of the fact that she dragged a leg and was exhausted because of having MS," Bea recalls. Selling lingerie was a good business, because the sailors and the shipbuilders were all making good money. "The store shelves were bare, and the housewives were delighted to have this opportunity to buy beautiful lingerie from my mom's catalogue."

The Crawford family also found other ways to make extra money. At country dances, Purdy would be outside collecting beer bottles for money, and he did a bit of clam digging, the hardest work of his life. In his teenage years, he worked for his half-brothers, who ran a portable sawmill around the small towns of northern Nova Scotia. During summers, Purdy did the hard work of pulling slabs of lumber off the sawmill's moving carriage. But he really yearned to be a sawyer, the master of the levers, who controlled the log cuts. A good sawyer was essential to the productivity of the business, and these skilled tradesmen were heroes to young Purdy. "Some guys could produce a lot more in a day than others. I used to dream I could be the great sawyer."

At times, he was so taken with the sawyer's life that his mother worried he might quit school and work full time in the sawmills. His brothers were good operators, successful men, but in her mind her youngest child, Purdy, the great surprise of her life, should be a professional, probably a teacher. Certainly, mining was out—Purdy could see the toll that kind of life had taken on his father. "I don't think I could do that; nobody would if they could," he says.

His heroes in those days were not just woodsmen but also ball-players. Baseball was big in the little towns of the Maritimes, perhaps inspired by the proximity of Boston, where sons and daughters often moved to find a better life and learned to root for the Red Sox. Purdy was a good second baseman but never in the league of those giants of northern Nova Scotia: the young men, mostly miners, who played for the Springhill Fencebusters. In the 1920s into the late 1940s, they were perennial champions in the provincial league. To this day, the stars of this team are vividly remembered: Gump Boss, the first baseman; Ackie Albion, a famous pitcher; and Purney Fuller, who struck out twenty-seven batters and still lost the game, according to local legend.

Purdy played ball for a while with a local team called the Londonderry Ironmen, an amalgam of players from various communities. One summer, a fellow came down from Collingwood Mountain, just to the north. A southpaw, he tossed some pitches to the team, and Purdy remembers flailing away helplessly with his bat. The phenom was Thomas Albert Linkletter, a.k.a. "Mountain Boy," and he was a rare triple threat—on the ballfield as a pitcher, on the stage as a fiddler, and on the dance floor as a quick-stepping strutter. "I would have loved to have been able to tap dance, play the violin, and pitch a baseball like Thomas Albert Linkletter," Purdy says.

This larger-than-life character enchanted the young Purdy, but education and a more serious purpose took over his life. The external force that propelled this inner purpose was his mother Grace, the first in a long line of formidable women in Purdy's life that includes his wife Bea, his law firm colleague Bertha Wilson, and his five daughters, all capable and articulate. From the beginning, he was gender blind—he simply did not see a person's sex as a criterion or an impediment to advancement. All around him, he saw young women he knew were being held back, including a cousin, Gracie Fife, who Purdy insists was smarter than he and who became a beloved teacher—a good profession, no doubt, but she was not given the option to do even more. He has always lamented that he was favoured for his sex while others close to him were denied the same opportunities.

His mother combined a passion for education, her family, and the Liberal Party—indeed, she no doubt instilled in Purdy his interest in politics, although his political allegiance has always been hard to pin down. He tends to support people, not labels. He might be considered fiscally conservative but socially liberal, and could be called a Red Tory or a centrist Liberal. He was Liberal by birth, but he has supported politicians of all stripes if they measured up. He admired Robert Stanfield, the revered Nova Scotia Conservative premier of the 1960s, has been known to give money to New Democrats, and is close to Nova Scotia Liberal MP Scott Brison.

The decision to go into law was no epiphany on the road to Damascus but a notion that was settling in gradually by the time he went to university. It was a way to improve himself—in fact, no one in his family had ever graduated from university. It was also a fascinating field and a focus of Purdy's curiosity. He had no thought then of a career on Bay Street or of becoming a CEO; he might perhaps become a country lawyer who dabbled a bit in politics.

The next step was admission to Mount Allison University in Sackville, about a two-hour drive from Five Islands. The Crawfords were United Church people, and Mount Allison had its roots in the Methodist Church, which in 1925 joined with breakaway Presbyterians to form the United Church. Even so, his parents were a bit worried that he might quit school. "At times I thought about it," he says. The major factor was his inadequacy in the French language. In grade 11, he had great marks but flunked French. In grade 12, he liked the French course, which emphasized reading, and he did well. But Mount Allison said he would have to bring his marks up, and he feared the prospect of writing another exam in French grammar—it was a test he knew he could not pass. One of the best days of his life, he says, was the day he was working in a sawmill, "when someone comes in and hands me a letter from Mount A that says they didn't see any need to write a supplementary in French." The lack of French has dogged him ever since, but he has never let it get in his way.

On his first day at Mount Allison, he met a lively talkative Cape Bretoner named John Buchanan. They would room together for three years. Buchanan figured Purdy would go far, either in business or in public life. "I recognized that Purdy was going to do something very very important with his life. I just didn't think I would—at that time." They were not alike, this odd couple of Mount Allison in the late 1940s. Purdy was a serious student, and John liked to have fun. Buchanan, nicknamed Hunk, had just escaped the protective cover of a strong mother, a widow raising a family without their father. He went a little wild at university, and it took him a while to get serious. Purdy, meanwhile, always serious, tried to keep John on the straight and narrow. It took a few years, but John got on course to become a Halifax lawyer and eventually Conservative premier of Nova Scotia for thirteen years.

Purdy might have been serious, but Buchanan insists he was not some dull stick. He liked the occasional adventure. One memorable occasion was an excursion by car with five student friends—including Buchanan and future federal MP Robert Coates—to the hockey arena in Charlottetown, a few hours and a ferry ride away. There, the hometown Islanders were hosting the visiting Sydney Millionaires. Buchanan, as a Cape Breton boy, was an avid Millionaires fan. The local PEI crowd was in an ugly mood. "The Sydney Millionaires were not just disliked by Charlottetown fans—they were hated. And I was caught up in the middle," says Buchanan. At one point, someone in the crowd recognized having seen Buchanan at the Sydney arena and shouted, "Hey, someone down there is a Cape Bretoner." According to Buchanan, "Purdy said we'd better rush to the Sydney bench because they were going to come after me." They got to the bench in time, and spent the rest of the game cowering behind the collective muscle of the Cape Breton players. Having survived, they raced back to the ferry but missed the last boat of the night. The gang of students had to sleep inside and beside the car in the cool night until they could board the ferry at 6:00 A.M. the next morning and get back to Mount A in time for classes.

Buchanan remembers his roommate as a frequent leader in discussions in the common rooms and dorm rooms. Purdy was interested in politics—not so much in partisan politics, but in political ideas. "I never got involved in those great philosophical discussions that he would be involved in," Buchanan allows. "I can see Purdy at his desk reading and reading; that is why he was so successful later in life—an abundance of knowledge in that brain of his."

Mount Allison in the late 1940s and early 1950s was a hothouse of young, rural people thrust together in dormitories and getting their first taste of the outside world—or, in some cases, just looking for a way to escape the restraints of straitlaced parents. One young student was Margaret Norrie, just sixteen and the daughter of a prominent Liberal family from Truro, Nova Scotia. Now Margaret McCain, activist, philanthropist, and widow of Wallace McCain, the New Brunswick french fry magnate, she remembers a great atmosphere with lots of post-class discussions of politics, sports, and changing social mores.

Margaret did not know Purdy well—but her future husband did. Wallace McCain was a hellraiser, and he was attending his third different university when he met Purdy at Mount A. They became friends, reuniting in later life when Wallace became a Toronto-based industrialist. Purdy was already dating his beloved Bea, the girl from Bass River, and Margaret recalls he wasn't in circulation as a potential date at the school dances. He didn't stand out for her crowd, she recalls, because "we didn't notice the ones with their noses in their books. He had a goal—he was there to learn and he accomplished it."

But she still carries the indelible image of a determined Purdy walking across the campus: "I can see him with his blond curly hair, his Mount Allison school sweater, and he always seemed to be walking like he was bucking the wind."

Bucking the wind, indeed. He was in his own world, commuting to Five Islands on weekends, hitchhiking down the country roads. During his final year at Mount Allison, he and Bea got married—he was twenty, she just eighteen. "It was what was done then—if you got into your mid-twenties and were unmarried you were an old maid," Bea explains. "And why not get married?" The two of them got to grow up together, and there is something to be said for that, she muses. Asked why he married so early, Purdy would say "I fell in love, with a girl from Bass River." When faced with that kind of opportunity, what was a fella to do?

John Buchanan remembers when Purdy came back to school, a newly married man, accompanied by his mother and his wife. In one of the common rooms, other students dropped by to say hello to Grace and Bea. One of boys said, "Mrs. Crawford, are you not concerned with leaving Purdy at Mount A with all the women here?" It was not certain which Mrs. Crawford was being addressed, but Grace Crawford spoke up: "Bea and I are not worried about that at all, because Hunk is going to look after Purdy." Everybody got a laugh out of that, knowing Buchanan's reputation for an easy-going lifestyle.

While Purdy finished his studies at Mount Allison, Bea stayed home in Bass River and worked as a telephone operator at the local exchange. Then Purdy won a scholarship to Dalhousie Law School in Halifax, where, in the three years, he stood first, second, and third in his class. He was part of a coterie of smart young law students, including Constance Glube, a future chief justice of the Nova Scotia Court of Appeal, Arthur Stone, another judge-in-the-making, and Saul Paton, who would make his mark as a lawyer in Toronto and whose recollection of Purdy was as a very hard-working student. Glube remembers Purdy well, but did not necessarily see him as a future business leader. She was aware that Purdy had a wife and needed help financially. She herself was married, and her husband was part of a successful family business. After second year, when she led the class in grades, she won a tuition scholarship and tried to pass it on to Purdy, who really needed it. The dean said it was outside the rules but assured her there would be some financial aid for Purdy.

In the meantime, Purdy had to work part-time to help pay the bills, and it was while working evenings at the tourist bureau in downtown Halifax that his loss of innocence came. At dusk one day, an African American man with a family came in looking for a place to stay, and Purdy found him accommodation at a motel just outside the city. An hour or two later, the man came back in a furious state—the motel wouldn't take him. Purdy felt inadequate to deal with prejudice. "I'd never been exposed to it before. I had sympathy towards him." He got another place for the family to stay, but it shook him to find such prejudice in his own province, home to a significant black community with roots dating back to the American Revolution.

While Purdy studied at Dalhousie, Bea, now in her second year of marriage, was the family breadwinner, having taken a community college business course that allowed her to work at the Moirs chocolate factory in downtown Halifax. It was a role she enjoyed and enabled her to dole out a living allowance to her student husband.

Their first home in Halifax consisted of one room with a bed and a hot plate. They soon moved to a better location near the university: a two-room attic apartment with its own bathroom. Then Purdy found a student apartment on North Barrington Street, which, they later learned, was not far from the city dump. When Bea walked in, the first thing she saw was what seemed to be a thick coat of flour all by the doors and on the top of everything. "I soon learned that this was cockroach poison because I would see these cockroaches running up the walls. I was terrified, but even worse, Purdy confessed that he already knew about the roaches."

The Crawfords survived the cockroaches, and after Dalhousie the couple moved to Boston, where Purdy, now ambitious and aware of his potential, took advantage of a scholarship to Harvard Law School. Harvard shaped him. It is where Archibald Cox, a leading labour law specialist and future prosecutor in the Watergate scandal, became his role model. He also studied securities law under the estimable Louis Loss. He worked hard and got even better marks than he had at Dalhousie.

The young couple found a support network as they settled into life around Cambridge, the Boston community that is home to Harvard. Typical of Maritimers, various members of Purdy's and Bea's families had flocked to New England in search of work, picking up jobs such as carrying ice to tenements or selling fish. Bea's aunt and uncle had a dairy farm just outside Boston, and the young Crawfords would often visit on Saturdays in time to catch the Perry Como show on television—the first time they'd had access to that medium. While Purdy attended Harvard, Bea worked in the office of a meat packing plant across the Charles River in Boston, where she mastered an early form of calculator called a Burlington machine.

Purdy regrets not spending more time enjoying Boston's arts and culture, but he did find time to play for the law school hockey team, where he gained a reputation as a smooth-skating defenceman. One of his teammates was future federal finance minister Donald Macdonald. More important, though, the Harvard experience and his exposure to people and ideas stoked Purdy's ambition, and he decided to practise law in a major centre. He considered New York, Boston, and maybe Toronto, but not Montreal, where his lack of background in Quebec civil law and his paltry French would hold him back. "I had a good feeling about Boston because people in Atlantic Canada always look to Boston," he says. But his hopes were dashed when he learned that, in that era, he would have to become an American citizen to get called to the bar in that country. He was also invited west to practise law in a Saskatchewan firm run by former Nova Scotians, and he could have become an academic. The dean of law at the University of British Columbia suggested a posting, but "I wanted to be on the firing line," he decided. That meant being a practising lawyer.

First, he returned to Halifax and articled under distinguished lawyer Roland Ritchie, who later would become a justice of the Supreme Court of Canada. Ritchie belonged to an old Halifax family, and his brother Charles was a diplomat whose rich and perceptive diaries, published in later years, became classics. Despite his august bloodlines, Roland Ritchie had a zany sense of humour. Purdy recalls fondly the day the dignified jurist wore a new suit to the office and, bending over to pick up something, split the pants up the rear—and laughed over and over about it. In the law, however, Ritchie was a serious man and later wrote the Drybones decision, a landmark Supreme Court ruling that upheld the authority of the Bill of Rights to override federal legislation.

But Halifax was too small a stage for Purdy, and New York and Boston were out of reach, so Toronto seemed about right. Ritchie gave him some contacts there, but with a certain hesitation—he and other Halifax lawyers warned Purdy that Bay Street would squeeze work out of him but never allow him to rise in the hierarchy. It is a classic concern of Easterners, that central Canada would never appreciate or reward the young men and women who flocked to Toronto or Montreal in search of opportunity. Purdy never bought that argument. He was ambitious and believed that talent eventually would win out.

Years later, he would be frustrated when young Maritimers told him that central Canadians just chewed them up and spat them out. As a mentor, he wrote one of his harshest letters to a young Nova Scotian who complained about the innate prejudice he encountered on Bay Street. Purdy's response: quit making excuses—do some hard work instead of whining. Hard work, he believed, was the great equalizer, and Purdy would become the hardest-working guy in Canadian law.

Purdy still has a lot of old friends in Nova Scotia, but he admits he lost touch with many of those he knew as a boy. For a lot of them, school had ended in grade 8 or 9, and they headed off to the woods or mines to work. He has thought about the forces that propelled him to seek a great career outside Five Islands while others were forced to stay home—or shied away from the challenges of a larger life.

He admits, too, that a good life was to be lived as a small-town lawyer or entrepreneur. As a teenager working in the sawmill with his brothers, he had found himself in Spencer's Island, a small community along the Bay of Fundy west of Parrsboro, and the place where the famous ghost ship *Mary Celeste* was built; her voyages left a trail of death and mystery right up to the day in 1872 when she was discovered abandoned on the Atlantic Ocean with no sign of her crew or their fate. In Spencer's Island, Purdy had chatted with local merchant and sawmill owner, Isaac Spicer, a smart man whose family had deep roots as shipbuilders, sea captains, and woodsmen. Years later, when Purdy was a practising lawyer in Toronto, he happened to meet Ivan Rand, a legendary judge and academic who had gone from Mount Allison to Harvard Law School. Rand told him the full story of Isaac Spicer—that Spicer had been in Rand's Harvard class but never practised a day of law in his life. Instead, he had returned to his hometown, on the edge of the Bay of Fundy, and was content to be a local businessman.

Purdy was both fascinated and haunted by Spicer's choice: why invest money and energy in a Harvard education only to become a small-town entrepreneur? Purdy could understand the longing for home, the security of a small community, and the comfortable life of a local big shot. But he found an answer to this quandary: he would bring the flavour of the Maritimes to Bay Street, by turning Canada's hard-driving urban business centre into a small town in which he would play a central role—as a kind of mayor, versatile fixer, and everyone's trusted confidant. Canadian business became Purdy's other Five Islands, where, on meeting someone, you inquired about their spouse or kids or parents, where you knew everyone and everyone knew you. And time after time, he would reach back into his past, to the friends he made in Five Islands or Sackville or Halifax, and they would be the most enduring and resilient relationships of his life.

## Chapter Two

# A Breeze Blows
# Up Bay Street

In the mid-1950s, if you practised law at Osler, Hoskin & Harcourt on the fourth floor of the stately old Dominion Bank building at the corner of Yonge and King in Toronto, chances are you were either an Osler, related to an Osler, or went to school with an Osler. Or you might be the son—but certainly not the daughter—of one of the firm's clients or the offspring of a senior partner. So what about this young outsider from Nova Scotia, who, despite his fancy Harvard master's degree, talked kind of funny and lapsed into the homey expressions of rural Nova Scotia? One senior partner was concerned about the way Osler's newest recruit came across, so he asked a more junior colleague to give young Purdy Crawford some help—in the form of a book of English grammar and usage. The kid from Five Islands was taken aback and sulked a little bit. "Maybe I felt offended for a day or two but I thanked him later," Purdy would say. He read the book, found it useful, and carried it with him. "It hurt a little bit at that time. I came to realize after studying the book that it was well worth it."

Back in Halifax, he had been told that Bay Street's elitist firms would work him hard but that he would never advance to the top.

Yet he was willing to take that chance with Osler. The firm had been resistant to change, so he felt it would have to alter its ways to survive. In a strange way, then, the book incident, though rude and insulting, suggested Osler's bluebloods could see a future for Purdy Crawford, this bright-eyed kid with the cowlick who talked of "Kweebec" and "fillett mig-non." And the slights, the small insults, never distracted Purdy from his goal of succeeding in the big leagues of Canadian law.

In fact, as a lawyer, he would always balance his two aspects— the Bay Street fixer and the rural rube. With the right audience— Alberta oilmen, Ontario iron miners, plain-folks investors—the rustic Crawford would appear, quite naturally and without pretence slipping into the colloquialisms and aw-shucks style of his youth. And because he was very smart, he could easily switch to the cocktail chatter of the bluebloods. Before becoming the country's top business mentor, he was mentored himself by the lawyers at Osler, and from them he learned the first lesson of mentorship: the truth can hurt, but get beyond the small slights and keep your eye on the horizon. Part of success is knowing your limitations, and all these decades later he is still concerned about the way he talks and writes. In later years, he depended on his assistant Sue Lucas, whom he calls a kind of mentor. "She used to tell me sometimes I wasn't writing the right way; she knew her grammar and knew how to talk to people."

In joining Osler, the young Purdy knew exactly what he was do-ing—it was the first of many strategic career moves. He had interviews with other big Toronto firms, and it would have been a thrill to work with the formidable Maritimer Alex MacIntosh at Blake, Cassels. But Osler was perhaps the snootiest of the old-line firms. Many of its lawyers were competent but not first class, and they were not bringing in new blood fast enough. The firm, Purdy concluded, was good, but it was running out of gas. It needed young people with accents even stranger and more exotic than his. The irony is that Purdy was stigmatized for his accent, but law firms now strive to employ as many accents as possible. They want to reap the commercial benefits of diversity, to appear worldly and progressive to bright recruits, and they know that, to flourish, they have to reflect their clients, who come from diverse ethnic and geographical communities.

Purdy's successful career on Bay Street was the product of a quick intelligence and natural sociability—but he also put in back-breaking hours of work learning to be a lawyer. Over the next decade, he would amass far more than the ten thousand hours that author Malcolm Gladwell says is the threshold for success by an "outlier"—someone who climbs to the top from outside the Establishment. But, as Gladwell also points out, it helps to be at a turning point, when the skills and traditions of the old are supplanted by a new paradigm. That happened in corporate law, as the business world changed and the old verities faded. Purdy Crawford arrived at the dawn of the era of the public company and a wave of takeovers, when client firms were changing partners, and of the age of the financing frenzy of junk bonds and derivatives, mutual funds, hedge funds, and private equity. He came along at the right time—and with the right combination of work ethic and street smarts.

But it took a while. The world Purdy and Bea entered in 1956—the world of Toronto the Good, run by a tight elite of WASP families—was a foreign one. The Crawfords were WASPS, too, but coming from the Maritimes they were very much down-market—almost immigrants of sorts—and even the bustle of Harvard Yard had failed to shake the Bay of Fundy sand off these two young people.

Yet the founder of Osler, Hoskin & Harcourt had himself been an ambitious outsider, like Purdy and Bea. Britton Bath Osler was the son of a former sailor and Anglican minister who immigrated with his wife Ellen from Britain to a rugged log cabin in a poor parish in rural western Ontario. There, in threadbare surroundings, eight children were born, but the family had some connections and huge ambitions,

26

and, in the opening up of Canadian society in the mid- to late nineteenth century, the children did very well. William became Canada's most acclaimed physician, another son, Edward, a prominent banker and stockbroker, and Britton Bath Osler founded one of the country's most prominent legal firms. Known as B. B., he began practising law in Dundas, Ontario, and eventually set up his own firm there before moving to nearby Hamilton. He became one of the top legal minds in Canada, and the federal government tapped him to prosecute the biggest case of the era: the trial of Métis revolutionary Louis Riel. It ended in a controversial guilty verdict, and Riel's execution in Regina and the debate over his place in history rages on.

In 1882, B. B. Osler took his act to the hurly-burly of Toronto, where he formed a partnership with John Hoskin and several other lawyers. He also teamed up with another upward striver named D'Alton McCarthy, but the McCarthy family later split from the firm, with D'Alton's son Leighton departing to form McCarthy & McCarthy (by the early twenty-first century, it had emerged as the megafirm McCarthy Tétrault). The Osler firm thrived on a sterling clientele led by names such as Inco, the dominant global nickel supplier, and Eaton's, the department store titan, and by forging strong links with some of the elite New York law firms, which sent business its way. But by the 1950s, the firm was experiencing the rigor mortis that afflicts family businesses in any industry that fail to draw on the expertise of outsiders.

Curtis Cole, in his fascinating history, *Osler, Hoskin & Harcourt: Portrait of a Partnership*, notes that all of the firm's twenty-two lawyers were white and male, and all but two were members of a mainstream Protestant church. The firm's first Catholic was called to the bar in 1954; its first Jewish lawyer did not join until 1963. And as for women, forget it—women were not considered appropriate for the world of gentleman's clubs, cigars after lunch, and firm, manly handshakes. Cole writes that, of the eleven partners, five were members of, or directly related to, the Osler family. Of the three men who joined the partnership on December 31, 1955, one was the son of a senior partner and another, Allan Beattie, was the son of the senior Canadian executive of the firm's largest client, Inco, which in some years contributed 30 percent of Osler's profits. Beattie, who grew up in northern Ontario, was an excellent lawyer, a wise and shrewd leader, and it was he who delivered the book of English usage to Purdy. It was indicative of the role he would play. Although both men had plenty of social skills, Beattie would take on the duties of tactful communicator to balance to Purdy's drive and ambition to build the firm. Beattie became Mr. Inside to Purdy's Mr. Outside.

In the mid-1950s, even the names of the partners suggested the atmosphere of a boys' school or officers' barracks: Brick and Campbell Osler, Mossy Huycke, and Gordon Wotherspoon, a much-honoured Second World War veteran whose military-style nickname was "Swatty." But the firm's management was almost exclusively in the hands of one man: a towering presence named Hal Mockridge, a great nephew of B. B. Osler.

Mockridge, an outwardly stern and exceptionally erudite man, was an excellent lawyer and, more important, his mother was an Osler. He had grown up in the United States, gone to Princeton, and learned to speak fluent Latin and Greek. As he contemplated his options, his uncle, Britton Osler II, talked him into taking up law and coming back to Canada. It was a great move for both Mockridge and the firm. Mockridge proved an astute leader, and his hiring the likes of Purdy Crawford showed not only that he knew the firm needed to change, but also that he knew he and his generation could not be the agents of change.

On moving to Toronto, the first hurdle Purdy and Bea faced was accommodation. Purdy found a bed in a University of Toronto frat house, while Bea shared a room at the YWCA with a friendly young woman who was working her way through school—although Bea was uncertain exactly how she earned her money. One afternoon, the two made plans to meet that evening for a spaghetti dinner, but the roommate told Bea she had to do a little business first: "I've got a trick at 4 and I should be ready at 6," the woman brightly informed her. Bea would later admit that "I didn't even know what a trick was."

The couple's separation did not last long, however, and the Crawfords were soon installed in their own apartment.

Purdy's transition at work was no less eye-opening. The firm operated in the shadow of Mockridge, who often made choices based on personal taste. Purdy remembers that Mockridge was on the boards of both Royal Trust, which was a good client of Osler's, and the Bank of Montreal, but because of business conflicts, he could not stay on both. Royal Trust was an Osler standby and a great generator of billings, but Mockridge wanted to stay on the Bank of Montreal's board because, well, he liked that board better. So he gave up Royal Trust and Osler lost an important client. Yet, the firm's senior partner never sought new business—new clients flocked to the great man. "He was a different style of lawyer," Purdy says. "Today, you gotta get out and hustle. Mockridge said to clients 'Come to me,' and they did, making a successful firm." It was a model built on relationships, but the model was changing. Corporate clients were becoming more demanding and the business more competitive. In that atmosphere, law firms would have to learn to pursue clients and work hard to retain them—business development would become a prized asset.

Purdy performed well at Osler and, in 1962, only four years after becoming a full member of the firm, rose to partner. He soon also became a member of the executive committee and a leader on the panel of Osler lawyers who recruited articling students. This latter role became pivotal in the rise of Purdy Crawford and critical for Osler, for it is the firm's recruiters who shape the character of the organization. He settled easily into a triumvirate that included Allan Beattie and

Fred Huycke, son of Osler senior partner Mossy Huycke. According to Curtis Cole, Purdy Crawford "was the big-picture visionary who provided much of the impetus for the firm's direction toward the future," while "Allan Beattie was the good natured manager of growth," and Fred Huycke acted as the anchor with the past.

The firm continued to maintain its long-time relationships, such as those with Eaton's and Inco, since it could provide expertise beyond what was available from in-house counsel. It was, however, a world very different from that of today—no buzzing BlackBerrys, but two-martini lunches in dark steak houses and gentlemen's clubs. For all of Mockridge's sternness, he could be a convivial colleague and a guide to the inner workings of the Upper Canada establishment. Peter Dey, a bright young recruit to Osler in the late 1960s, remembers working with the then-aging Mockridge one morning, and as the lunch hour approached, Mockridge suggested they repair to the exclusive Toronto Club. They settled into the lounge, where Mockridge ordered a double martini and Dey, a novice to sophisticated imbibing, asked for a beer. When it came time to walk upstairs to eat, Mockridge, in his trademark gravelly voice, advised, "Peter, you can't fly on one wing." So, Dey remembers with fondness, "he had another martini and I had a beer." Mockridge became Purdy's mentor both in law and in other aspects of being a senior partner. The Mockridges took the Crawfords under their wing, to give them guidance on dinner parties and social gatherings. The Crawfords were being groomed.

For a while, Bea worked in the contract department at the stockbroker A. E. Ames, where she continued to use a Burlington machine to write up contracts. She loved working on Bay Street, but after a year, "I became heavy with child [their first, Suzanne, born in 1957], and in those days when maternity clothes became necessary one was expected to leave gracefully. From this time on I became a housewife." As the children kept coming—six in fifteen years—Bea admits, "I was a bit of a single parent and I didn't mind that. It was easier to make a single decision than two."

All the while, Purdy was emerging as a major force in changing the culture of the Canadian legal scene. His rise at Osler was a watershed in the firm's move from a family compact of elite, private-school-bred lawyers to a meritocracy. David Johnston, now Canada's governor general, saw that transition as an articling applicant to Osler in the 1960s and later as a legal scholar. Inside Osler, he said, Purdy would join other young lawyers in their thirties who pressed for change. "Osler was one of eight or nine old-line firms, managed and led by older men, and very much an aristocracy. It was who your family was, and whether or not you went to private school was important." But these new men—and, later, women—democratized the articling-recruiting process and based advancement on talent alone. That marked the transformation of Osler, which was ahead of the curve on "the Street." Over the next ten to fifteen years, law firms that clung to the old ways diminished and those that embraced meritocracy flourished. Purdy's rise, Johnston says, was the beginning of that new era.

Meanwhile, Purdy gained an important ally in the form of an articling student named Bertha Wilson, who would become the first woman to be an Osler partner and later the first female justice of the Supreme Court of Canada. "It took a lot of pushing and pulling to hire Bertha," Purdy says. Indeed, it did. Bertha Wernham was born eight years before Purdy, in the Scottish town of Kirkcaldy, also known as the birthplace of the intellectual father of capitalism, Adam Smith. After university, where she trained as a schoolteacher, she married a young clergyman, John Wilson, and joined him in a small rural parsonage in Scotland. They then emigrated to Canada, to a congregation in Renfrew, in the Ottawa Valley. John became a naval chaplain in the Korean War and later was posted to Halifax. As John continued his naval service, Bertha enrolled at Dalhousie law school. The dean first dismissed her as a young wife and dilettante just passing her time, and suggested, in words that are now famous, "Why don't you just go home and take up crocheting?" But she won him over with her serious intent and devotion to scholarship. She became a top student and made the acquaintance of a young Nova Scotian named Purdy Crawford, who was a couple of years ahead of her in school.

After law school, Bertha articled with a Halifax firm, but when John left the navy in 1957 to take a job as a church fundraiser in Toronto, Bertha went to Bay Street looking for an articling position for the Ontario bar. She was lucky that, the day she came to Osler, Hal Mockridge was in New York on Inco business—Mockridge did not see a future for women in the law. But Swatty Wotherspoon liked her mind and took note of John's naval service. He told her to hang fire on other interviews, and then set about convincing the other partners. Purdy was one of those who strongly supported her hiring, and in time Mockridge came around, but only for articling. It was understood she would be out of the firm in a year.

She quickly became a lawyer's lawyer, advising other solicitors on their briefs and becoming a specialist in legal research and knowledge management—far ahead of her time. The firm still didn't see this female lawyer as out in the world meeting clients, but, as Curtis Cole points out, her relegation in fact became a source of Osler's competitive advantage. Wilson became an innovator, helping change the firm into an intellectual champion on Bay Street just as law firms began to realize they had to shift from relationship-based law to knowledge-based law. And she overcame her detractors because she made the firm money. "Mockridge didn't like her coming, it was a different age," Purdy explains. "He was very negative about hiring a woman; but six months to a year later, she did some work for him. He was so impressed, his views on women and the law changed."

One day, Swatty Wotherspoon called her into his office to describe an assignment he knew she would love to get immersed in. She interrupted him, saying she could not do it—her articling year was up and she had to find another job. It did not take long for a decision to be made: she was officially a member of the firm. It took nine more years before she became partner, but by that time she had a huge reputation as the mind behind Osler.

Purdy and Bertha became a team. He relied on her for research and for her knowledge of the law, while he was out finding business for the firm. Asked whether he mentored Bertha Wilson, he insists it was the other way around: Wilson mentored him in a lot of the law. She did that for a lot of lawyers. One of her innovations was a central memo system which allowed lawyers to retrieve information efficiently from previous cases and judgments that could be used to prepare current cases.

Wilson's biographer Ellen Anderson, in *Judging Bertha Wilson: Law as Large as Life*, describes her role: "It is generally accepted that Purdy Crawford, Allan Beattie and Bertha Wilson—none of them related to the founding Osler family—did the most to bring about reform in Osler's management structure." Crawford, she says, was the rainmaker in bringing in new business, and Beattie the consolidator and consensus builder. As for Wilson, she became known, initially, as the in-house lawyer's lawyer and then as a profit generator in her own right. It was testament to her stature that young lawyers, if they were going to be hired, would have to do one research paper for Bertha.

But Wilson was also being courted by governments looking for smart women to appoint to the bench. In 1975, Purdy was working on a deal involving the purchase of hotels by two of his best clients, Richard Shiff and Ken Field, the partners behind the Bramalea real estate organization. As usual, he was leaning heavily on Bertha Wilson. One afternoon, the two got together in advance of a big meeting with the clients. They talked for a couple of minutes, and then Bertha said, "Purdy, I can't go on. This afternoon, it is going to be announced that I am going to the Ontario Court of Appeal." Purdy's mind was entirely focused on the meeting ahead, and for one of the few moments in his life, he was ungracious. "My initial reaction was not as warm and bubbly as it ought to have been." It would take some time to undo that—"it was more the look on my face. It was stupid." The relationship survived, however, and they would remain friends as the woman from Kirkcaldy rose to the Supreme Court of Canada.

As he matured as a lawyer, Purdy Crawford came to believe that big, all-involving—and even low-paying—assignments can change your life. That has been his advice to his young students and acolytes, and his own career is a striking demonstration of his own rule.

He started out wanting to be a labour lawyer, an interest that grew out of his university experience—he had been deeply influenced by teachers at Dalhousie and by Archie Cox at Harvard. And he started off at Osler working for a number of companies on their labour files. For many smaller companies, he negotiated their first labour contracts. "The biggest challenge was getting your own client to be reasonable, and take off your necktie, and relate to the guys across the table." Purdy could do that.

One of Osler's clients was the Canadian subsidiary of US icon Bethlehem Steel, and Purdy was given the labour file for the company's big iron mine in Marmora, a village about two and a half hours' drive northeast of Toronto. The job involved absorbing the big settlements involving the US parent and its unionized workers, and adjusting the agreement for the Canadian workers in Marmora. Purdy would go down to Bethlehem's corporate head office in Pittsburgh to get briefed, then drive up to Marmora, where he encountered miners who resembled his father Frank and found he could relate to them. It was great training for a young lawyer. He recalls that one of the Bethlehem executives was a disciple of Ayn Rand, whose raw individualism had a following in the corporate world. He gave Purdy a copy of one of Rand's door-stopping novels, but it didn't catch on with him. What did catch on was a reasonable knowledge of how corporate benefits worked and of the intricacies of pension plans. That understanding would serve him well in years to come.

But labour law could be frustrating. He was hired with the expectation of handling the Inco labour file, but he was part of a crowded team that included a trio of lawyers from the Osler family and another senior partner. He was often bored by being handed the small grievances or technical points in the contract. The model of lawyering on the labour side did not appeal to him—senior partners hoarded their clients and used younger professionals for drudgery, instead of bringing on younger people and establishing their credentials with the client firm. The Bethlehem file was one of the few where he got his teeth into the law and got to work with the client. The lessons would resonate long after, when he became a senior lawyer himself.

Frustrated, he began to move into the broader area of corporate law, and began working closely with Hal Mockridge. It was a thrilling collaboration, which saw Purdy's evolution from labour lawyer to mergers and acquisitions and corporate lawyer. In the still-small firm that Osler, Hoskin & Harcourt then was, he came to see himself as a generalist within the broad ambit of corporate law. In his later career, he would watch as lawyers deepened their specialization. "I see guys at Osler's who do just loans for banks or act for borrowers from banks and that's all they do. I'd go up the wall with such specialization. It is inevitable and more efficient and better for the client," he admits, but he would not like being so narrow.

Yet it was a landmark assignment in one area of the law that made his career. It is hard to know the precise moment when Purdy Crawford, the bright, young up-and-comer, became Purdy Crawford, the dean of Bay Street lawyers. But it had a lot to do with becoming the go-to person for an entire section of the law.

Purdy's rise accelerated with his appointment as staff lawyer for the Kimber Committee and the writing of groundbreaking securities

legislation that rolled out of that: It was a time when Ontario securities laws were glaringly out of date, and to prepare for reform,
the Ontario government in 1963 appointed a committee chaired by
Jack Kimber, head of the Ontario Securities Commission (OSC), and
graced with star corporate lawyers Bob Davies, head of a dynamic
corporate law firm, and Hal Mockridge from Osler. (They were later
joined by figures such as mutual fund pioneer Warren Goldring and
economist and future academic leader H. Ian Macdonald.) The two
lawyers brought along young stars as committee staff: Howard Beck,
an up-and-coming lawyer with Davies's firm, Martin Friedland, a
legal academic and future dean of the University of Toronto law
school, and Purdy Crawford, the young partner from Osler.

The committee was responding to a time of upheaval. There was
continuing scandal around the shameless promotion of penny mining stocks, which had become an ignominious Canadian tradition.
Controversy raged over whether new issues should be sold through the
public markets, giving rise to fraudulent promotion. Insider trading
and the regulation of takeovers had become front-page issues, particularly in light of allegations surrounding curious trading by brokerage
firms in the days leading up to Shell Canada's bid for Canadian Oil
Companies in 1962. Then, in 1964, after a flurry of insider trading
in its stock, Texas Gulf Sulphur reported a massive copper and zinc
strike around Timmins, in northern Ontario. That game-changing
discovery set off an orgy of speculation involving mining companies
with claims in the area of the great find.

The most spectacular case involved the run-up and collapse of
the stock of Windfall Mines, a speculative junior controlled by Viola
MacMillan, a legendary and respected prospector, and her husband
George. The boost in share prices was attributed to the MacMillans'
manipulation of information, and the case eventually ended up with
convictions for both of them. As the scene unfolded, the scandal
placed a heavy burden on the Kimber Committee to come up with a

blueprint for a new securities law that would protect investors. The Windfall scandal shook Bay Street out of its complacency, exposing the potential for mind-bending fraud and insider trading. The stakes had risen beyond the petty stuff.

The Kimber report was a seminal moment in Canadian securities law, says Howard Beck, who grew to admire the tousle-haired young Maritimer who worked alongside him on the committee and then in writing the new rules. This one project became the wellspring for Crawford's and Beck's five decades of leadership in the securities law field—indeed, it shows how public service and private advancement are intertwined and how an appetite for hard work paid off for the Nova Scotia kid who never played fast and loose with facts but was always the best prepared person in the room.

Jack Kimber, an engaging man, was the collegial hub for the committee's work, Beck recalls, as the team would meet outside normal working hours. "Mockridge and Davies were major guys, but everyone revolved around Jack, including Purdy, Marty, and me. We met three nights a week with Jack, and it was the personality of Kimber that was central. Purdy was outstanding as a lawyer, and Jack was the glue that got people there." Beck understood that "it was more difficult for Purdy because he was married and had children, and I was a bachelor." He notes that "Bea is very accommodating and it is a great relationship. If his wife wasn't supportive he couldn't have done what he did, not only in the Kimber Committee but in Osler's and the spin-offs from that experience."

When the report was issued, Crawford and Beck were commissioned to draft the legislation. Purdy remembers it as intellectually stimulating but not highly remunerative—he got his law firm salary and nothing more. He had started at Osler's at $400 a month, and by the time of the Kimber Committee he was up to $500 to $600. "It was volunteer time," he says, yet "it's one the most significant things that happened to me in the development of my career."

Whenever a new and complicated securities issue came up at the OSC, Harry Bray, the commission's long-time regulatory champion, would say "why don't you get Purdy Crawford to do this?"

The results of this work were tougher rules across the board and stronger powers for the OSC as watchdog. According to historian Christopher Armstrong in his book on the OSC entitled *Moose Pastures and Mergers*, "[t]he main thrust of the bill was to ensure fuller and more accurate disclosure for investors. Propectuses would contain greater detail; public companies must make financial disclosure every six months; investors would have a chance to scrutinize proxies and takeover bids. The OSC was being given much more authority over the [Toronto Stock Exchange]."

The final legislation did not meet all expectations because primary distribution through the stock exchange was not banned, but the province's attorney general promised that the problem would continue to be closely studied. The new law got a generally positive response, but there were concerns that the tough new rules would not be applied uniformly across the country. Ontario was the primary jurisdiction for securities law—it was home of the biggest stock exchange and the heart of corporate Canada—but each province and territory had its own regime. On that basis, the new act sparked a court challenge from business interests. The challenge failed, but the issue underlined a continuing lack in Canada of a national securities regulator, which created an inefficient compliance system and confusion among global investors about who spoke for Canada. It was not a theme that the Kimber Committee tackled, but it would engage Purdy for the rest of his career.

For David Johnston, legal scholar and future governor general, the broader impact of the new securities legislation lay in its role as an economic document, tipping capital markets regulation slightly away from the British tradition toward the American model. "It modern-ized Ontario and Canadian economic regulation in capital markets, using the efficiency and innovation of the United States but without the excessive regulation of the US," he says. Meanwhile, he adds, "it preserved something of the British tradition of less detailed legislation and more fundamental principles." According to Johnston, it was a significant landmark in Purdy's career because "he or she who holds the pen controls what happens afterward." It was the beginning of a life of high-profile policy work. "And Purdy was not a one-trick pony. He was doing it all the time—in commissions and law reform committees. He would always be involved himself, or encouraging other people."

Johnston became the embodiment of the Crawford model of career advancement. He was a product of Purdy's knack for picking and mentoring great talent and helping guide it to good decisions. And even if the individual left Purdy's orbit at Osler, the mentoring established a relationship that he could draw on, for the good of his acolyte, for the advancement of Purdy's own philanthropy and public service, and in the best interests of Canada.

Johnston, who hails from Sault Ste. Marie in northern Ontario, went to Harvard, where he captained the ice hockey team and was the model for Davey Johnston, the hockey-playing character in the book and movie *Love Story*, and to Cambridge University in England for a master's degree. In the mid-1960s, Johnston, back from Cambridge, showed up on Purdy's door because he needed an articling position on his way to a career of legal scholarship. Purdy, impressed, upset protocol by signing him on the spot and expected him to join the Osler firm the following spring. But Queen's University, where Johnston was studying, wanted him to teach that year, and he had to send Purdy his regrets. Crawford didn't take it personally—he could see the talent. So he left the offer on the table while inviting Johnston to come just for the summer and work on drafting the new securities legislation arising from the Kimber report. "He had no reason to show any interest in me," Johnston says. "He had offered me a job I expected, but I didn't take it up." Johnston points out that he still hasn't taken up the articling position that Purdy has left open for fifty years. He jokes that Crawford once ended a letter of reference for Johnston by saying "you'll be lucky if you can get this man to work for you."

With Purdy's help, however, he got a privileged chance to watch Crawford and Beck at work, labouring through the evening drafting legislation. Johnston admired what he saw in Purdy: "A superb professional with a strong sense of justice in crafting this economic legislation with appropriate balance of interests. I admired his professional skills and sense of idealism in improving the law. His capacity for work is unusual."

The Kimber Committee would be a landmark for Purdy and for Bay Street. Beck would go on to become a senior partner at the firm which became known as Davies Ward & Beck, later to merge with another big firm and maintain its status as a powerhouse, now known as Davies Ward Phillips & Vineberg. Purdy, meanwhile, would lead Osler to new heights, laying the basis of the firm which today boasts close to five hundred lawyers and has a knack for hiring the biggest game-changers in corporate law, including superstars such as Peter Dey, Brian Levitt, and Clay Horner.

It was indicative that old truths were dying, and Osler was poised for a different kind of leadership. As evidence, some point to 1969, when the company's oldest and most valuable client, Inco, became embroiled in a bitter strike by its workforce. The strike lasted 128 days and demanded huge efforts by the Osler labour team. It ended with a big settlement, and the vote by the bitter Inco workers passed by a whisker. Inco was not happy. Shortly after the settlement, the company moved its labour business to a hard-charging labour specialist firm named Hicks Morley and its leader Robert Hicks. It was a huge blow to Osler—and evidence that the old loyalties no longer held.

In this changing world, Osler needed a boost. Purdy is frank about his role: "I changed the paradigm in terms of recruiting. I was in charge of student recruiting early on. Life was straightforward: I could go out and hire students who impressed me. For two or three years, Osler had a one-up on other firms in terms of recruiting." Using his hard-acquired expertise from the Kimber Committee, he also taught securities courses at law schools and got close to leaders at the University of Toronto, Osgoode Hall, and Dalhousie law schools. Purdy joined an all-star team in building a ground-breaking corporate finance cluster at the U of T law school. The team, firmly grounded in legal practice, also included David Johnston, Jack Blaine from McCarthy's, future Supreme Court of Canada justice Frank Iacobucci, and another future jurist, Jack Ground from Osler. Wherever he taught, Purdy loved the interaction with scholars and students, and they became part of his vast pool of candidates who, in the years to come, would change the face of Canada's legal profession.

From that moment, it took a different set of credentials to succeed in the legal world. By the late 1960s, Hal Mockridge was planning his exit from an executive role. Meanwhile, his son Britton—a direct descendant of the firm's founder—was coming in as an articling student and, as he prepared to join the bar in 1969, the executive committee was determining if he would be invited to be an associate lawyer with the firm. Mockridge excused himself from the deliberations, historian Curtis Cole notes. The son did get admitted as an associate, but left after two years. It was a signal: Bay Street's family compact era was over; the Purdy Crawford era was in full swing.

Chapter Three

# RAINMAKER

D eborah Alexander was a wide-eyed, small-town girl out of
eastern Ontario, who went to University of Toronto law
school and ended up articling at the venerable Osler law
firm in the mid-1970s. To her surprise, she was given a mentor, and
that was Purdy Crawford, a senior partner and the firm's leader—if
not in title, at least in spirit. She was intimidated by the great man's
reputation when she stepped into the Osler premises at the corner
of Yonge and King and sought out her new boss's corner office.
"You come from a little town and you go into his office and see the
windows on two corners. But then there is this big friendly bear of a
fellow, who is totally charming." Alexander became one of Purdy's
most successful projects at Osler, setting the foundation for a career
that has taken her to the senior legal post at the Bank of Nova Scotia.

She owes that to Purdy, who served as career counsellor and life
coach, to the extent of helping her develop strategies to deal with
sexual harrassment. And he became her role model as a steel core inside
a velvet glove. The charm never left, but she could also see the mettle:
"I saw how tough and strong he was. I worked for him for five years
and in situations where I felt the hair going up on back of my neck.
He is a tough negotiator, I thought, and he never compromised on
principle, values, family."

She came out of law school wanting to be a litigator, but he pulled her into corporate law, and she became a pioneering woman in that still very male world. He also taught her how to go out and get clients because, after all, he was the consummate rainmaker in an era before that term even became popular. He was different from Mockridge, the brilliant magnet for business who was so good that people would flock to him. Mockridge and his senior partners would heap scorn on any firm, like perpetual rival Tory Tory DesLauriers & Binnington (now Torys LLP), that would actually market itself. Such shameless huckstering was unseemly, the old guard felt. The idea was to inherit old clients or attract new ones through the force of reputation. But that was no longer enough. Now, you had to go out and get customers. Client firms were merging like crazy and the old Establishment was crumbling. And for the new wave of CEOs, one law firm's name held no more mystique than another's—when the wooing began, old allegiances meant very little. Osler's reputation was sterling, so it managed to hold on to many of its traditional clients, but it depended on Purdy to drive its growth.

George Vesely, a Czech-born engineer who veered into law, joined Osler as an articling student and would scan the sheets of new client actions—the lists of cases that were being added to the firm's roster. Each file notation began with a partner number, indicating the senior person on the file, followed by a slash and the list of other lawyers. He noted that, almost invariably, the partner would be No. 16, which was Purdy Crawford's number. Big clients, small clients—he was bringing them in. Tim Kennish, a corporate lawyer who came under Crawford's spell, remembers that "he was a bit of a whirlwind, he generated a lot of work, and just about everybody got involved with work he was creating." Deborah Alexander says, "when I worked with him, he was a transaction fellow. He never had the title chairman, but everyone knew, unless moving office chairs, that that person you needed to get onside was Purdy."

Crawford was never a courtroom lawyer—he would show up in that role only twice in his career and it wasn't to his liking. The courts were frustrating places because of all the procedural delays. He preferred the role of trusted counsel who could cut through bureaucracy and double-talk to get things done. And he saw the law firm as a generator of constant outreach: lawyers on commissions, lawyers writing articles, lawyers delivering speeches, or teaching law courses. These interactions were great recruiting tools and terrific business development instruments, but Purdy also saw Osler as an intellectual force on the street. It was not just a billable-hours machine but a distinctive culture of curiosity and knowledge—and that was very much part of Bertha Wilson's legacy as well.

According to Peter Dey, from the early 1970s on, Crawford defined the culture of Osler, Hoskin & Harcourt. "There was a focus on professionalism of a high quality, but also a public spiritedness that really made my life and others' so interesting. We were always encouraged to develop issues of policy. He made it fun and he gave encouragement to do legal writing and commenting." It also gave Dey and other young lawyers a brand of their own that they could take out into the world.

As the firm grew, it spilled out of the old Dominion Bank building, which had become the Toronto-Dominion Bank building after the merger of the two banks in the mid-1950s. In the 1960s, Osler moved across the street to the twenty-storey Prudential Insurance building. That would be its home for about fifteen years until 1977, when it moved onto the sixty-sixth and sixty-seventh floors of towering First Canadian Place, the new headquarters of the Bank of Montreal.

That physical growth was emblematic of Crawford's business development prowess. In the mid-1970s, Brian Levitt joined the firm, and he noted that Crawford was one of the ruling triumvirate at Osler, along with Alan Beattie and Fred Huycke. "But Purdy was in ascendance. We started working together, and he was good at developing people. He was the sort of person who was interested in getting the business and only doing the business that made sense for him to do"—which meant his team of junior lawyers got close to the client.

According to Dey, he created the template for the modern law firm. "He was very focused on growth—that turned him on. Attract the clients, get them comfortable with him and then, with a junior like me, he would hand the client over." David Allgood, another of Purdy's Osler acolytes and later to become general counsel at the Royal Bank of Canada, says the understanding was that these clients were not Purdy's clients—they were the firm's clients. A lot of law firms were just conglomerations of sole practitioners, but Osler was truly a partnership in all its aspects.

Yet all this conviviality masked a toughness that Crawford displayed when he encountered behaviour he did not welcome. A lot of people on the Street have felt the cold Purdy treatment, the eyes boring in on them, the flat-out declaration that "we are not doing it this way." Crawford was not into loud histrionics or desk-pounding anger, but, if irritated, he could freeze people out. "You were either loyal to him or you weren't in the program," Alexander recalls. "I have heard him say 'he is not on my team.' It wasn't that he didn't appreciate an opposing view, but it was about your conduct and whether you are part of the team. When a team makes a decision, you implement it and don't keep undermining the team. He was very loyal and expected the same, and he worked incredibly hard." There were people in the law firm who did not measure up, although Purdy, ever gracious, would never categorize them that way in public. But as the firm grew, it couldn't afford senior people who were making a lot of money but weren't contributing. They would be encouraged to leave, perhaps to find positions on the court, with a client company, or on their own. It would be traumatic at Osler, but the new guard wanted to give space to more productive people, and it was never personally motivated. Often, it was the ever-gracious Alan Beattie who delivered the bad news in the nicest possible way.

Starting in his early years with the firm, Purdy's great gift lay in a shrewd and dogged recruiting of talent. The story of Bob Lindsay is a case study in the pattern that Purdy would follow time after time. Lindsay is an amiable guy with a sunny disposition, a steel-trap mind, and an obsession with tax. He is, in fact, a total tax geek, and Purdy pursued and won him for Osler, thus creating the vital building block of the best tax law team on the Street. At many firms, the tax team is relegated to the back room, but at Osler Crawford brought the tax professionals out front—he saw tax as a centrepiece of good corporate law.

The romancing of Bob Lindsay started in the late 1950s, when Lindsay, a Toronto boy with an MA in economics, was on his way to Dalhousie law school and met a young Dal graduate named Purdy Crawford. They kept in touch and, on Lindsay's graduation, Purdy pitched him on joining Osler. But Lindsay was determined to go to Ottawa to become a tax expert with what was then called the Department of National Revenue; later, as a fully formed expert, he planned to dive into private practice.

Just as Purdy was in the right place at the right time on securities law, Bob Lindsay was graced with exquisite timing on tax. After his stint with Revenue Canada, he was seconded to the Department of Finance during the wave of tax reform in the late 1960s and early 1970s. An accountant named Ken Carter had headed a Royal Commission that proposed a top-to-bottom overhaul of taxation. It was radical reform and, although watered down somewhat by political forces, it is essentially the law we know now. Lindsay ended up as the principal draftsman of the tax reform, which came out in 1971. Lindsay lived and breathed it, working round the clock seven days a week so that he hardly knew what day it was. Lindsay would wake up in the middle of the night vexed by a tax problem and scribble notes to himself. In the morning, all would seem so logical, and he would write the law.

When Lindsay was ready to enter the private legal world, all the major Toronto law firms with tax departments wooed him, in the way hockey or baseball teams compete for high-priced talent. Some threw money at him, but Purdy Crawford was always in the back of his mind. And the Osler lawyer was intent on making contact. On one of Purdy's journeys to Ottawa, he ran into twin brothers John A. and Jim Tory and Jim Baillie, leaders of the hard-charging Torys firm, at the airport. He wondered if they were trying to recruit Bob Lindsay. It turned out they were: Torys had rented a suite at the Château Laurier hotel and the firm's senior people had laid on a sumptuous meal for the young bureaucrat. But, Lindsay says, "the reason I went with Osler is Purdy—here is a guy who is not just well regarded, but such a nice guy." Lindsay joined Osler on the first day of 1972, and he built a tax team in the same way Purdy built the firm: get the best people, get them on the right track, sit back and let them practise law, and don't monopolize the clients for yourself.

Purdy was not Lindsay's mentor in tax law; with tax reform, it would mean relearning the law, which now required specialization as never before. So Lindsay got to run his own show. Crawford remarked to Lindsay that, as a corporate lawyer, he spent 25 percent of his time on tax, but when he saw the complex new legislation, he knew his time had to go down to zero or up to 100 percent, so he took it down to zero. Another nail in the coffin of the generalist lawyer.

Out on the street, there was a broad agreement with Purdy's statement that "because I hired so well, Osler got a one-, two-, or three-year advantage over other firms who were good." But it was also because he developed the talent he brought on board. Bob Lindsay could be left on his own, but Purdy became a kind of watchful, indulgent babysitter for a bunch of other whiz kids. Peter Dey, a forceful, high-energy personality, often needed to be toned down, but Purdy

admired the younger man's vitality. Deb Alexander needed to be given
pep talks and to gain a better understanding of the business world.
Bright young things came and went—including Paul Martin, who
swung through Osler on his way to a business career and, ultimately,
the jobs of finance minister and prime minister of Canada. Ace litigator
Edgar Sexton came on board from another firm and thrived. Hockey
goaltender Ken Dryden, embroiled in a season-long contract dispute
with the Montreal Canadiens, did an articling stint at Osler; in his
final months, he had goalie mask designs arrayed around his office.

Tim Kennish had been hired by Hal Mockridge, but found himself
working a lot with the always-accessible Crawford. Kennish started
out as a broadly based corporate lawyer but enjoyed the occasional
foray into antitrust law. Purdy encouraged him, saying this would
become a hot field in the coming decades. So, when Canada drafted
a new competition law in the 1980s, Kennish was already prepared to
make competition his career. He owes a lot to Crawford's prescience.

Dey was another disciple, an Ottawa boy who, like Purdy, had
gone to Dalhousie and Harvard. When he showed up in Toronto in
the fall of 1967, he did the rounds of a half-dozen firms and had offers
from all of them. What clinched the deal was Crawford's offering to
give him credit for his Harvard graduate degree—the whopping sum
of $100 a month. And Purdy had the clout to make the hiring decision
on the spot. Recalls Dey: "Here was this guy from Five Islands in this
large establishment law firm, and it was a measure of his influence at
this stage in his career that he could say 'we've got a guy here...'."

The hiring game also stoked Crawford's competitive fire. In the
final phase of hiring Dey, Purdy was up against the legendary Arthur
Pattillo of Blake, Cassels. Dey finally told Pattillo he was going to
Osler. "Arthur said, 'one pup deserves another,'" Purdy says, with
the competitive gleam still in his eye. Dey remembers Crawford's
uncanny ability to place the right people in the right places. Dey had
been with the firm only a few months when he got a call from the

Ontario government—the OSC wanted a study on mergers and had asked Purdy to suggest a research director and a general counsel. He put forward David Johnston as counsel and Dey as research director. The two worked with OSC director Harry Bray and produced the landmark merger study.

"That was Purdy giving me a steer, and when I came out of that project, I was perceived to have an expertise in securities law," Dey says. It was the start of a path that would lead to Dey's stature as one of the top securities lawyers of his generation, chairman of the OSC, author of a landmark study on governance (*Where Were the Directors?*), and on to a career in investment banking, private equity, and as a dealmaker.

The young lawyers also benefited from just spending time with their mentor. They would gather in his office for law talk, but Purdy was a busy man, and they would soon learn the cue to leave was when he said, ever so gently, "I won't keep you." But, Dey adds, "I've also seen him with an edge. He knows right from wrong and if something is not going in the right direction, he will draw a line."

Deb Alexander says she could see the hard resolve at the core. If you want to succeed in business law, Purdy told her, you have got to be able to speak to clients who live in a world of numbers, and so you should relate to income statements, balance sheets, and debt-to-equity ratios. Purdy is not impressed with people who don't understand the fundamental importance of tax and accounting in business. He urged Alexander to read *Forbes*, *Fortune*, and other business magazines and gave her exercises to learn about companies. He told her that, every time she did a securities offering, she should read the notes to financial statements before anything else. And Alexander was a willing pupil—if this was a hurdle to getting ahead, she figured she would be stupid not to do it.

And she also got advice that transcended the law. Despite the groundbreaking work of women like Bertha Wilson, the business world of the 1970s was a misogynistic environment. Alexander encountered situations where harassment was a common threat. Clients drank too much and made remarks and gestures that today would probably result in legal charges. Knowing the limitations of the harassment law in those days— and the implications of accusing a client's employee of bad behaviour—Crawford and Alexander would talk about ways to manoeuvre out of situations before they got out of control. At functions, Purdy advised Alexander always to stand with her back near a wall so heavy-breathing lechers couldn't ambush her. She learned to cajole bartenders for pseudo-martinis that were nothing but water. She learned to leave an event gracefully by saying she had to get something from the cloakroom and not coming back. "When people go for that extra drink, you get into a cab and go home. It was about managing through stressful situations. Most important it was 'you do it and don't create a scene'." Alexander passes on those same rules to today's young lawyers as preventive tactics: "I tell women, you can put yourself in vulnerable positions or avoid them altogether."

His young lawyers also loved Crawford's coolness under fire. People at Osler tell a story—given the mists of memory, or discretion, the client's name is not disclosed—that, in fact, might be an amalgam of incidents that have melded together in the minds of the participants. It was a very large transaction, probably on behalf of a major mining client, and most of it was tax driven, involving a corporate reorganization and a big public offering. Then, two months later, it came to light that the tax opinion was wrong—not only had the Osler team missed it, but so had two accounting firms and another law firm.

The lawyers knew the error had momentous consequences for the client, with potentially huge liabilities, and some were offering to fall on their sword. Purdy had been out of the office on an appointment when the mistake was detected, and a nail-biting Alexander waited for him by the elevator. Purdy came out of the elevator doors, saw the expression, and said, "Oh, dear, what's the problem?" Alexander explained the situation and that the tax people were ready to resign. She recalls Purdy's response: "I will not hear that—we are all in this together, and I will get it fixed." Already, a big pension fund was threatening to sue. So Crawford booked a plane to Ottawa that day and took some of the Osler lawyers with him. After conversations with federal officials, it was deemed that the tax decision fell within the spirit, if not the precise wording, of the law. In fact, the law was actually amended—problem solved.

"The thing that stuck with me is it didn't matter what went wrong, it was 'we,' 'us,' and there was no yelling, no recrimination," says Alexander. "There are so many ways in life you can break people by the way you respond to their making mistakes, but he bore the burden of angry clients. His leadership skills were outstanding."

George Vesely, another rising star of the Crawford years, remembers a similar situation—perhaps the same situation—regarding a file in which he was involved. "A big mistake was made, the kind of mistake that could have been embarrassing internally and externally, and all kinds of bad consequences could have flowed." But there was never a witch hunt. No one resigned, and two weeks later a solution was found. "In any other law firm, it would be a question of: who caused this problem? And people would be fired. Purdy did not look for scapegoats."

Vesely remembers as a first-year partner going with Purdy to a meeting of clients. A legal point came up, and Vesely knew his senior colleague had command of the law on that point. But instead of taking the floor, Purdy told the group: "This is too complicated for me. Why not let George deal with this?" "Very few people would want to be so selfless," Vesely says. "He put my interest, in developing my career, ahead of his own. He had no ego." Because of that spirit, "I am one of the generation of people who would go through fire for Purdy."

Perhaps the most significant hire of this period was Brian Levitt, whose low-key style and ironic wit mask a razor-sharp mind. In the old Osler law firm of the 1950s, neither Levitt, who is Jewish, nor Alexander, a woman, nor Vesely, an immigrant, would have been hired. But Purdy could see only the talent. Levitt was recommended to Purdy by David Johnston, who had taught him at law school. In Levitt, Johnston unearthed one of the top corporate law minds and a business leader—a bit like Purdy Crawford himself.

Levitt had gone to the University of Toronto to take engineering and had become a friend of a bright young fellow named Ed Clark, who was studying economics. The two bonded and, after university, Clark headed off to do a PhD while Levitt went to law school, articled at Blake, Cassels, and tried the role of country lawyer in Shelburne, Ontario. But he didn't fit into small-town law and lost interest. He found himself temporarily out on the street.

Then came a call from his friend Ed Clark, who had become a federal bureaucrat with the wage- and price-setting Anti-Inflation Board (AIB), a controversial creation of Prime Minister Pierre Trudeau after he had campaigned in the 1974 federal election *against* wage and price controls. Clark told Levitt the AIB needed people and that it was interesting work, and Levitt moved to Ottawa. As part of his job writing regulations, Levitt worked on pricing for lawyers and ran into senior people at Osler. Encouraged by them, he showed up in Toronto and, on David Johnston's recommendation, Purdy hired him. Levitt thrived under his older colleague's career development approach: bring in the business and let the young lawyers take over the client work.

As a rainmaker, Purdy landed some big assignments: not only old faithful Inco, but also jobs for Molson, Imasco, and Coca-Cola. The old Osler firm had a client list full of private companies and Canadian subsidiaries of US giants but wasn't really involved that much with publicly listed companies. And it didn't need to be; the public company was not such a big factor in that old economy. That changed in the 1970s, as the publicly traded entity, with its access to cheaper capital, became the focus of expansion and change, and

Purdy was well positioned to move Osler into this new market. He also maintained close relations with Wall Street law firms, which allowed Osler to win a lot of cross-border business, a big plus as the continental economy began to integrate.

And he signed up the federal government. The late 1970s and early 1980s witnessed an upheaval in Canada's energy policy, and Osler was hired to deal with one of the most complex corporate restructurings in Canadian history. Dome Petroleum had been a rocket in the 1970s under its visionary leader, Calgary oilman Jack Gallagher, who had a stomach for debt and a skill in attracting federal support as a national champion in frontier oil development. But in the 1980s, as high interest rates and a plummeting oil price took their toll, Dome's house of cards folded and the firm fell into bankruptcy protection, weighed down by debt of about $6.3 billion to fifty financial institutions. Ottawa tapped Crawford to act as a special advisor, but he turned to Brian Levitt for most of the on-the-ground work. Levitt didn't mind—it was the way the firm operated. "It was an interesting job—not much law involved, but we were acting for the government and they were just trying to be present and stabilize the banking system," Levitt recalls.

Sorting out Dome turned out to be a key chapter in the Purdy story and a precursor of what he would encounter at AT&T Canada and then in the ABCP fiasco. The federal side of the Dome restructuring was driven by deputy energy minister Mickey Cohen and his assistant, Ed Clark, Brian Levitt's old friend. Purdy gained an indelible impression of Clark's mastery of complex detail in the Dome reorganization. Those three men, Crawford, Levitt, and Clark, would become major actors in Canadian business over the next forty years. Typical of Purdy, he was the hub and built spokes of friendship and mutual respect. It was networking, yes, but it was also about building widening, intersecting spheres of influence through mentoring, charitable giving, and lawyer-client roles.

The assignments got bigger, but, in some essential ways, Purdy did not change. He kept his roots in Five Islands and the Maritimes. In those days, he could count on a month of summer holidays, and he and the family would head down home. At first, they would stay with relatives; later, they bought a place of their own. Purdy would lay low and play golf three or four times a week in Parrsboro with his Maritime pals. And as his star rose in central Canada, he became an important contact for Maritimers, sitting on boards of private and public corporations down east and pulling young Atlantic Canadians into the maw of Bay Street.

Meanwhile, his family kept growing. After Suzanne, born in 1957, there was Heather (1960), Mary (1962), David (1963), Barbara (1965), and Sarah (1972). Amid this burgeoning brood, Bea gave him a lot of room and peace of mind. She ran the home, even as far as home maintenance, for Purdy was hopeless about any kind of technical chore. Despite Purdy's teenage fling in sawmill operations, it was Bea who could hammer a nail with accuracy. The children remember one incident when their father madly punched buttons on what he thought was the TV remote, until Purdy discovered he had been attacking the wrong device—the garage door had been going crazy.

He was home most nights and tried to be engaged in parenthood. He had no separate office to which he would retire. Instead, he would settle into a big chair to read, listen to family issues, and grab a quick nap before suddenly lurching back into the family conversation. Purdy never viewed himself as a workaholic because he could leave work behind and get totally absorbed in the children or lose himself in a great book.

Bea, too, never saw him as a workaholic because he enjoyed his work so much—he was a "work-is-fun-aholic," she likes to say. That was better than working long hours and coming home to complain about what he was missing in life. Rather, Purdy thrived on the work, got home most nights, and the kids were there. There were also stressful times, however, like the big real estate deal which he finally wrapped up at 10:00 P.M. on Christmas Eve. The family understood— as he came in the door, daughter Heather handed him a martini.

It helped that he was a morning person who would get up at five or so and do some reading before slipping into the office at seven o'clock. "By the time the world got up, he had been reading briefs, books, and newspapers," remembers Joe Martin, a management consultant who became his back-fence Toronto neighbour and close friend. Purdy figured he could get a quarter of a day's work done before anyone came around to his office—and he could grab a power nap as needed during the day. He took up golf and even dragged some initiates out to the course to show them how to play. "He batted left, which was unusual," Peter Dey recalls, "and he loved needling me—he constantly reminded me I was losing my hair."

On summer Saturday mornings, Purdy, the early riser, would be on his way to some golf course as the sun came up. In her late teenage years, daughter Heather admits there were mornings they would meet as she was coming in the door and he was heading out. It was typical of the Crawfords. There were not a lot of rules—the children would find their way, and the parents would provide good examples. There were tough times, as in any family—Suzanne, the eldest, was critically ill as a child—but the family overcame them.

Friendship is important to Purdy, and one of his deepest, most enduring relationships has been with David Johnston, the close-but-no-cigar Osler lawyer whose energy and brainpower propelled him up the academic ladder. David and Sharon Johnston lived a peripatetic life and, with their five daughters, spent a lot of time with the Crawfords as they changed homes, cities, and jobs.

Crawford and Johnston were working together in the late 1970s as members of the Adams Committee, a groundbreaking inquiry into the accounting industry. The Johnstons made a rule not to travel on the same plane, so that, if it went down, one of them would survive to look after the children. What's more, "we had it written in our will that, if we died in a common disaster, the Crawfords would adopt our children, and they agreed," David recalls. The two couples—Purdy and Bea and David and Sharon—ended up at a conference in Banff, where the men were discussing the Adams report. This time, however, on the flight home from Calgary, all four were on the same plane, which was hit by lightning and quickly dove several hundred feet— "although I thought it was three miles," Johnston says. "It is going down, and I look at my wife and the Crawfords. All our planning of what would happen for our children is going for naught—this is the end." But the pilots righted the plane, and it landed in Regina for safety checks before heading on to Toronto.

In the mid-1980s, Purdy Crawford was in his early fifties and had been at Osler for more than a quarter-century, and the law firm he had built was in very good shape. Deb Alexander had just been made a partner, but she still depended on Purdy to bring in the business. One day, she was called to a partners' meeting. "I walked in, and they are talking. Purdy sat at the big table and I sat opposite him. He looked up and had these notes and a strained look—he suddenly realized he had not spoken to me. He started on the speech on why he was leaving Osler, and I burst into tears. I ran out, with Brian Levitt chasing me all the way down the hall." She wailed, "Why? How? This can't be happening to me!" Later, she said, "I was just devastated."

Purdy was leaving Osler to become president of Imasco, the Montreal conglomerate that was one of the firm's corporate clients. Crawford later came to Alexander and said he was sorry, but she was inconsolable. "What am I going to do?" she blurted out. So he levelled with her—if she wanted to do this kind of corporate work, she had to go out and find it herself. "He insisted I wouldn't just be someone who did work for other lawyers. He was the one who said 'I want you to go out and do it'." And so it started: the cold calls, the lunches, the constant hunt for clients—the things her mentor used to do. She became a top lawyer, with her own slate of clients and, in time, Bank of Nova Scotia came calling, and she became its general counsel. That was Purdy's legacy, too—he was ready to cut her loose, and it was liberating.

George Vesely was also distressed, convinced that the firm would fall apart, but Purdy insisted the time was right for him to leave. In his view, a number of corporate law partners—Levitt, Dey, Jack Petch—had been under his shadow and would now step up to become leaders, and the firm would be even better than before. "When Purdy left, each of these guys developed into very big names in corporate law," says Vesely.

Janet Salter was a young lawyer who came to Osler in the wake of Purdy's departure. The Osler team that recruited her said that other law firms were trying to capitalize on his departure, but they insisted the firm would not suffer from the absence of Purdy Crawford. They were trying to get ahead of the issue. Privately, there were worries inside the firm that its links with fifteen to twenty major clients might be frayed by Purdy's leaving. And Salter would hear the stories of how he walked the halls and knew the names of the lawyers' spouses and kids. Certainly, no one had that pivotal a role after Purdy, but still the firm kept getting bigger.

The lesson: great leaders are distinguished not by the huge hole they make on departing, but by the team of people they have developed to succeed them. Osler didn't die after Purdy left, far from it—it flourished, and that might be his most enduring gift to the firm.

Chapter Four

# The Montreal Years

I n 1985, Purdy Crawford was at the top of his game. He was a trusted advisor to CEOs, rainmaker to a major law firm, and mentor to a galaxy of young rising-star lawyers. Why did he give up that comfortable life to take a risky run at becoming a corporate CEO? Because he had a hankering to manage a company, and there was an offer on the table. "My motivation in joining Imasco was simple: I would not leave practising law unless I became a CEO—and there it was."

Senior lawyers often yearn to sit in their client's chair, making the big strategic decisions, but few actually take the leap. It is not unusual for CEOs to have law degrees or for lawyers to join their client companies as internal counsel, but it is quite another thing to go from heading a top-ranked legal practice to running the business of a big client company, as Crawford did. And the record of lawyers who take over operating companies is spotty. Lawyers are narrow and legalistic in their focus, as specialists in areas such as securities, property, tax, or trusts. CEOs have to have a wider perspective and chart strategy in an organization with a lot of moving parts. Lawyers are often risk averse, the natural outcome of years of keeping their clients out of trouble. But CEOs have to take risks to grow companies; they have to take on debt to accumulate assets. Susan Wolburgh Jenah, a Crawford protegée and, until fall 2014, head of the Investment Industry Regulatory

Organization of Canada (IIROC), agrees that what it takes to be a good lawyer is different than what it takes to be a CEO. A lawyer doesn't always see the big picture—the forest for the trees. "Purdy was always the kind of lawyer who didn't get caught in the trees. He was about the big picture and it made the transition easy."

Of course, some successful lawyers have become successful chief executives. John A. Tory (the late father of John H. Tory, the former Ontario Conservative leader) went from working with his twin brother Jim at the family law firm to serving as wise *consigliere* to Canada's richest family, the Thomsons—a role that included being president of the media-information company and, at various times, managing energy and travel assets. Indeed, John A. Tory's and Purdy's stories have striking parallels that extend beyond the Tory family's historical Nova Scotia roots—they were both trusted advisors who moved to the corporate firing line.

Crawford, though, was not your typical corporate lawyer. His public fame came from securities law, but he could see how the corporate financing piece fit into the big picture. He was a generalist, not a narrow pedant, and he was a voracious reader on business of all kinds. His favourite bedtime reading was not some legal journal, but the *Harvard Business Review*—or a biography of a business or political leader or military strategist. His study of business meant he often knew more about a client company than its in-house lawyers and felt he could, for example, run Inco about as well as many of its CEOs. Besides, Imasco was the cream of Canada's corporate crop. In terms of profitability, it was one of the top dozen companies in Canada, a well-oiled machine that epitomized the modern conglomerate. Its management was highly decentralized, so that Purdy could manage the big picture, and he would not have to know every minute detail of each of its operating subsidiaries. He would hire the best managers and give them a lot of freedom—although he admitted later that he could have used more operational experience.

Peter Dey suggests the secret of going from lawyer to CEO: "If you are a natural leader, the switch can be fairly easy, and Purdy was very much a natural leader." Also, he suggests, Crawford was a people person, and a lot of the Imasco businesses, from pharmacies to tobacco and fast food, were retail businesses. Crawford was a retail kind of leader.

Purdy had not been a big consumer of Imasco's landmark products, Player's and du Maurier cigarettes—he never smoked cigarettes, although he liked to join a colleague in lighting up a cigar at the end of the day. But, like John A. Tory at Thomson Corp. (now Thomson Reuters), his personal association with Imasco had been long and mutually rewarding. About a decade earlier, the company's CEO and long-time builder Paul Paré, looking for new board members, had come to Osler's Toronto offices to ask Crawford to join. Crawford agreed and began to develop an influence that transcended the typical director's role. Indeed, he became the very model of how a gifted outsider can move to the decision-making inner circle. Ottawa lobbyist Torrance Wylie remembers that Purdy was *un homme de confiance*—a right-hand man—to Paré. Wylie himself would join Imasco and, as Purdy came on board as CEO, become a valuable *homme de confiance* to Crawford.

And Paré was hungry for advice. Imasco's roots can be traced back to 1912 and the formation of Imperial Tobacco Canada, which, by the late twentieth century, had emerged as one of the dominant cigarette companies in Canada, with about half the market share. Paré had witnessed a lot of this growth. He joined the law department of Imperial in 1949 after serving as a lieutenant-commander in the navy and graduating from McGill law school. After a stint away from Imperial working for a competitor, he was lured back to an executive job in 1964, just as all hell broke loose in the tobacco industry after the release of the US surgeon general's report on the dangerous health effects of tobacco use. The devastating verdict changed the game in the tobacco industry, and although Paul Paré, like all the industry leaders, would argue with some of the report's findings, he knew it was a new world for Imperial. The company was a sturdy money-maker, and smoking would remain a big part of our culture for decades, but it would never grow as it did in the past. Tobacco was not a banned good, but the surgeon general's report was the beginning of a long litany of disincentives to sales, along with ever-higher taxes, health warnings on packages, restrictions on advertising, and the ultimate blow: the loss of the sports event sponsorships which had been Imasco's stock in trade, including the high-profile Canadian round of the pro tennis circuit.

Seeing a progressively cloudy future, Paré decided to reinvent the organization as a diversified holding company that would use the cash still flowing from tobacco to fund expansion into other industries by buying well-managed companies that could exist on their own but with Imperial providing cash and clout. It was also the golden era of the conglomerate, when it was fashionable to build vast collections of companies which had little connection to each other but which would benefit from the strategic oversight and financial tools of a well-capitalized owner. And, the idea went, spreading a company over several industries would provide a measure of economic hedging—if one industry went in the tank, others might be at the top of their cycles. Hence, the business celebrities of the 1960s and 1970s tended to be ruthless empire builders such as Harold Geneen, the fabled meglomaniac at colossal ITT, and Tex Thornton, the relentless builder of Litton Industries.

Paul Paré was also an empire builder in his own way. By 1969, he had become president and CEO of the new holding company, Imasco, whose main holding was Imperial Tobacco Canada, but it was also undertaking an ambitious foray into diversification—initially in the food business. It acquired processors and marketers, but with mixed results. Imasco kept looking for acquisitions, despite scrutiny by the Foreign Investment Review Agency (FIRA), which monitored all foreign investments. The problem was that Imperial had been founded as an 83 percent subsidiary of what had become BAT Industries, the British tobacco group. The BAT stake had since fallen to just over 40 percent, and the British company did not have a representative on the Imasco board. Still, FIRA refused to treat Imasco as a Canadian-controlled company.

Even with this limitation, by the 1970s and early 1980s Imasco had made dramatic moves into retailing and fast food, and it had a stellar reputation as a conglomerate that more or less worked. But as Paré reached his early sixties, he faced two hard facts: Imasco still garnered 90 percent of its profits from tobacco, and there was the question of who would succeed him as CEO. He had two internal candidates in mind, but these well-laid plans blew up when one heir left the company and the other was deemed not to measure up. Paré looked around and saw someone on his board who knew the business inside out and had the gravitas to replace him. That was Purdy Crawford.

As a director, Purdy had been intimately involved in Imasco's diversification, helping Paré in the acquisition of Shoppers Drug Mart and working on the takeover of US fast-food contender Hardee's. In 1985, Purdy became president and chief operating officer of Imasco and the following year replaced Paré as chief executive officer. For all Purdy's knowledge of the company, he faced a vertiginous learning curve, not so much in strategy, where he was well prepared, but in ground-floor operations. Although Imasco was one step removed from its subsidiaries, Crawford still had to immerse himself in enough of the nuts and bolts to assess his lieutenants' capabilities— and he found it demanding.

The other challenge was geographical—he had to move to Imasco's head office in Montreal after living for almost thirty years in Toronto. He and Bea loved their north Toronto neighbourhood and their home on one-block-long Ansley Street, where the neighbours were all friends, doors were left unlocked, and a game of road hockey was always on the go. And the new Montreal appointment revived an old bugaboo: no matter how hard he tried, he could not learn French. In Montreal, he hired a French instructor who came early in the day, but to Crawford it brought back too many memories of grade 11 and struggling with French grammar. It was one thing he never really mastered.

He could manage the language issue as a CEO—after all, Imasco's business operations were continental in scope rather than Quebec-based. But language became a troubling issue when he moved outside the company to take on a community role as chairman of the United Way's Centraide fundraising campaign. Purdy excelled in fundraising and saw community volunteerism as an almost sacred duty. This was where he honed many of the skills that made him the most successful fundraiser in the corporate world. Some of the Centraide initiatives from that period still enrich Quebec society. But he was always afraid that, at meetings, the conversation in French would roll on without him and that the issue would have already been dealt with by the time he had a chance to speak. He would take his francophone assistant to meetings, to make sure he didn't embarrass himself, and she would monitor the talk and keep him from making major errors. Again, it was a little humbling, but Purdy always kept an eye on the big picture. He emerged as a tireless volunteer for Montreal charities, and he was proud of his role in establishing Centraide's 1, 2, 3 Go! project for early childhood education, a program still active in Montreal.

The Imasco job also meant a crushing amount of travel. He had been a bit of a weekend father back in Toronto, but now family time became even more scarce as both Purdy and Bea dealt with the demands of being a "power couple." Still, it was a good time for the move. Sarah, at fourteen the youngest of the children, was the only one of the six who moved to Montreal; the others were in university or already launched on their own paths. Sarah was admitted to a private school, the first time any of the kids had studied outside the public school system. And Bea, a warmly social person who revels in human contact, became a vital cog in the Crawford machine as letter-writer extraordinaire who kept tabs on friends and family.

"Our home life was never the same as it had been on Ansley Street," Bea recalls, and Sarah, she says, missed the safe harbour of a large family. She did, however, find some of that spirit in the home of her friend Sharon, one of the five daughters of Sharon and David Johnston, who was now principal of McGill University. Bea also filled the void by taking training in palliative care at McGill to prepare for volunteer work at the palliative care unit at the Royal Victoria Hospital, developing a new circle of friends along the way. She became even more indispensable for Purdy as he worked to master the Montreal business world—in essence, she was head of business development for the Crawford family. After going to a party, Bea would immediately prepare index cards about the people they'd met. "I do not have a photographic memory, and we were meeting so many new people," she says. "I often needed just a little nudge to give us the proper recall—'Mary Smith: pretty with lovely short blond hair, loves to laugh, has four children, summer trip to Europe, met at Bell party.'"

And there were a lot of people to keep track of. By the time Purdy came on board at Imasco, Paul Paré had developed four pillars of the company: the traditional Imperial Tobacco business; retail (Shoppers Drug Mart, United Cigar Store, Den for Men); restaurant (Hardee's and Burger Chef); and a much reduced food unit. By the late 1980s, the *Globe and Mail* observed, "Imasco has had interests in food processors (including the makers of Grissol bread sticks and Unico tomato paste), sporting goods retailers (Collegiate Sports Ltd.), dry cleaning (Embassy Cleaners Ltd.), soft drinks (Pop Shoppes International), office coffee service (Red Carpet Coffee Service), gift shops (Cavalier) and oil and gas (a 21 percent stake in what is now Canada Northwest Energy Ltd.)."

The takeover deals had been a bit hit and miss, as typical in the conglomerate game, but on balance, Paré probably had batted about .500—an average that the old second baseman Purdy Crawford could appreciate. But the transition beyond tobacco was not happening fast enough in Paré's eyes. After hitting some singles and doubles, he wanted home runs, and Purdy was given that mission. The goal was wholly owned companies with a dominant market share, strong, proven management, and an emphasis on retail and consumer operations.

One of the most promising assets Purdy inherited was Hardee's, a fast-growing burger chain with roots in Greenville, North Carolina, and founded in 1960 by Wilber Hardee, a pioneer of the fast-food concept, along with McDonald's Ray Kroc and Wendy's Dave Thomas. It was an instant hit, and the chain experienced explosive growth. By the early 1970s, the chain had attracted the attention of a pension fund manager at Imasco, who started investing in it and was doing very well. Imasco's corporate chiefs couldn't help but notice. In 1975, the year the chain opened its one-thousandth restaurant, Wilber Hardee sold out, his protegé was named CEO, and Imasco bought more than a million shares of its preferred stock. The conglomerate then proceeded with a creeping takeover which culminated in 1981, when Hardee's became a wholly owned subsidiary of Imasco. At that point, Hardee's systemwide sales exceeded $1 billion.

But the chain's growth had stalled by the time Purdy became CEO, and Hardee's was facing challenges. Gone were the days when customers would flock to any burger joint you put up. There were new entrants into the game and some older ones, such as McDonald's and Wendy's, were on the march across the continent. "The industry was maturing, and it had become increasingly competitive," Purdy recalls. Hardee's began eying a chicken chain called Roy Rogers, a brand built on the image of the popular TV cowboy and owned by the Marriott hotel group. As Imasco plotted the takeover, it used the code name Trigger for the project, echoing the name of the cowpuncher's trusty horse. But once inside the Imasco stable, Roy Rogers misfired—the mixing of the Roy Rogers and Hardee's brands was ill conceived, and Imasco decided to dump its ailing fast-food operations. In 1997, two years after Purdy's retirement as CEO, Imasco sold Hardee's for US$327 million—not a great price, but Purdy says Imasco didn't lose money.

The takeover of Shoppers Drug Mart was a more satisfying story. This was a deal Crawford knew well, having worked on it as a director. Shoppers' roots go back to 1921, when a Toronto druggist named Leo Koffler opened his first pharmacy; twenty years later, he handed the business over to his son Murray. Murray Koffler proved a great entrepreneur, revolutionizing the industry by introducing self-service in a pharmacy and building the Shoppers Drug Mart chain, with each store owned by an individual pharmacist or associate. He took the Shoppers system across Canada; then, in 1978, Imasco bought it. Koffler stepped back from the business, and Imasco was instrumental in promoting David Bloom to the CEO's job in 1983. Bloom had begun his career with Shoppers in 1967 as a pharmacist at the store in the large Yorkdale shopping centre in north Toronto, and within a year had become the pharmacist-owner at that location. He joined Shoppers' headquarters in 1971 and won several promotions. Three years after becoming president and CEO, he was given the chairman's role as well.

Bloom was one of Purdy's favourites, a manager who could run the company independently and provide a strong strategic hand with minimum oversight from head office. While Bloom was CEO, Shoppers expanded from 400 to 837 stores, sales quadrupled, and earnings grew tenfold. Bloom was the architect of a retail juggernaut that, under his successors, continued to grow well after Imasco exited the scene. As a measure of its success, Loblaw would pay $12.4 billion to bring the pharmacy chain into its fold in 2013.

In time, Paul Paré was able to persuade Ottawa's investment review people that Imasco was a Canadian company, and he began to look in earnest for domestic acquisitions that met his criterion: they should provide 10 percent of Imasco's earnings very quickly and grow from there. In 1983, he took a shot at buying Canadian Tire with a $1.1 billion offer but was turned away. And he continued to troll for acquisitions south of the border. He uncovered another fast-growing retail business: Peoples Drug, based in Washington, DC, the sixth-largest drugstore chain in the United States with 598 stores, heavily concentrated in the mid-Atlantic area. In March 1984, just before Purdy joined as CEO, Imasco paid US $320 million for the company. Peoples had been assembled by its president, a sixty-year-old visionary named Sheldon (Bud) Fantle. Starting with two stores in 1951, his company, Lane Drugstores Inc., had acquired the larger Peoples chain in 1976. Now combined with Imasco and working with Shoppers, "we hope to build the largest drugstore chain in North America," said Fantle, who would remain the head of Peoples. Those words would haunt both Fantle and Imasco.

It was, Purdy acknowledges, a bad move. As an unwieldy amalgam of about eight chains that Fantle had assembled, Peoples had a much different business model than Shoppers, and the stores were all company owned, without a pharmacist-owner on the ground. Culturally, it was incoherent and sleepy. Imasco started looking for solutions and, in the late fall of 1986, decided that the firm's builder, Fantle—once heralded as a brilliant leader and partner—would have to go. As Imasco's new CEO, Purdy would have to do the deed.

Purdy was not known as a great firer of people, although he had done it. Worse, he respected Fantle as an entrepreneur. It was late in the year, and Purdy reasoned that the worst time to do it would be before Christmas, so he decided to wait till the New Year. Purdy spent the holidays in agony, mentally preparing himself for the act. In early January, he flew down to Washington, DC, met Fantle at his club, and told the entrepreneur he was through. Fantle was very upset, left the table, and said he would be back shortly. Purdy waited for the longest forty-five minutes of his life, then walked out of the club. Fantle never came back. "It was not one of my better stories," he says.

Fantle's firing did not save Peoples, as Imasco scrambled for solutions. It parachuted David Bloom into the US company on a part-time basis with a mandate to get management fired up and position Peoples as "a consumer-driven company." But Bloom couldn't work miracles, and eventually he recommended that the chain be sold. Imasco got a decent price. Sometimes, managing is knowing when to cut and run, Purdy concludes.

Ironically, the one part of the business that needed little attention was Imperial Tobacco. It was a cigarette juggernaut, and it pretty much ran itself. Purdy says it had the best management team in the industry. It was part of a tight circle of tobacco companies which controlled a cash-rich but increasingly regulated market, with a highly controversial product under attack by the medical and health communities worldwide. But it also enjoyed very high barriers to entry from the outside. It was a cash cow, although it had an uncertain future in a western world that was turning against its product.

Purdy, meanwhile, was dealing with major shareholder BAT, which was undergoing its own transformation as it tried, like Imasco, to diversify beyond tobacco into areas such as financial services. Purdy felt secure, though, in dealing with his masters in London. "I always felt that we were the best performing company that BAT had a major interest in and they would leave us alone—and they did." Purdy would meet with BAT CEO Sir Patrick Sheehy each year, often over a round of golf in the United States. They went over Imasco's annual plan, and it was a good story: "There were times we were 40 percent of BAT's total earnings." Occasionally, the British company would complain about the costs of Imasco's acquisitions, but the relationship was mutually respectful.

All the time, the company kept a good handle on government relations. After years of Liberal rule, the Tories took over in Ottawa in 1984, creating some nervousness about whether Imasco would face greater scrutiny because of its partial British ownership. But a new foreign investment bill maintained its status as a Canadian company, providing lots of room to troll for assets. And Imasco wanted something big and Canadian.

It looked at the fastest-growing sectors and the biggest companies in each sector. A consultants' study came up with three potential targets: media, construction management, and financial services. Media were off limits and construction was unfamiliar ground, so Imasco settled on financial services. The big banks were out of reach because of rules that put a 10 percent cap on individual share ownership, so Purdy focused on the largest financial services company of which an outsider could legally acquire control. That was Canada Trust, an innovative and scrappy bank-in-all-but-name operating out of London, Ontario, and headed by an aggressive, prickly genius named Merv Lahn.

## Chapter Five

# OF TRUSTS AND TALENT

When Purdy Crawford came calling, Canada Trust was already the great disruptor of Canada's financial services industry, an upstart that was blowing up the industry model with a consumer-oriented focus that bordered on heresy. It more closely resembled a supermarket than the oligopoly of staid and rigid temples of commerce that Canadian banks still persisted in being. And it exhibited a marketing flair that, in one telling example, promoted its automated teller machines under the maverick-style— and irreverent—label, "Johnny Cash."

Crawford believed that Canada Trust's strategy could be summed up in one word: hustle. He gives the example of the time when Merv Lahn, in late spring one year, called his team together and said he wanted to start banking on Saturdays. In the stuffy oligopoly of major banks, Saturday banking was still a no-no. The Canada Trust management team said it could get the job done in a year, but Lahn said he wanted it done in a few months, by September—and it was. Try that at one of the Big Five banks.

The only problem was that Canada Trust had just recently been acquired by another Canadian conglomerate called Genstar, which itself was a complex cocktail of a company, a collection of building materials, waste management, and land development companies.

Genstar had been founded in 1951 as the Canadian offshoot of a Belgian bank holding company, Société générale de Belgique, with a mandate to get into construction and construction materials business in a Canadian economy that was soaring in its postwar urban development. By the late 1970s, according to James Lorimer in his book *The Developers*, Genstar "probably ranks among the most important dozen corporations in the country in the sheer scope of its economic power."

Genstar's rotating duo of CEOs, Ross Turner and Angus McNaughton, ran the company with considerable independence and had moved the company's operating headquarters from Montreal to San Francisco. Like Imasco, Genstar was on a diversification blitz, branching out into financial services, and its major acquisition was Canada Trust, which Genstar merged with the already acquired Canada Permanent. The relationship between Canada Trust and its new owner, however, was tense. Lahn, as Canada Trust's builder, did not take kindly to outside direction and preferred to get rid of Genstar's ownership. Imasco learned that two of Genstar's largest shareholders, Société générale de Belgique and the massive Quebec pension fund Caisse de dépôt et placement du Québec, were unhappy with Genstar's management having moved the company's base out of Quebec and taken steps to protect the company from takeovers.

Imasco went ahead with its offer and, with the backing of major Genstar shareholders, captured the company. "There was some push and shove and then a bear-hug ending," says Torrance Wylie. It was Crawford's first megadeal as a CEO and he loved it. His best moment at Imasco was "the night we locked up Genstar to get Canada Trust. It was around midnight, an exciting time, and we were justified." It was an outstanding acquisition, and Merv Lahn proved to be a difficult but capable leader. Lahn had hoped that Ottawa would extend the 10 percent ownership cap to protect his near-bank. But he didn't get what he wanted and, after a disagreement with Imasco, retired in 1990, making way for his hand-picked successor, Peter Maurice. Lahn died in 1994, a great builder who changed banking in Canada.

Then there was the battle to get the deal approved by Ottawa. It was a long slog. The federal government was concerned about any deal that mixed industrial and financial assets and was reeling from a crisis in Canada's trust industry, which virtually imploded because of risky real estate loans. As a result, most of the industry, with the notable exception of Canada Trust, had been folded into banks. But Imasco committed not to blend Canada Trust into its industrial and retail operations, to maintain a separate board, and to keep a semblance of public share ownership through a class of preferred shares, which satisfied Ottawa's concerns.

It was hard enough doing the deal, but then came the unbundling of Genstar, as Imasco proceeded to sell off the parts it didn't want. Purdy was lucky—he managed to sell the unwanted pieces ahead of a recession that would have trimmed his cash intake. But the part no-body wanted was Genstar Development, a land development company with property assets in some of the key urban centres of Canada and the United States. The mid-1980s was a tough market for residential real estate, particularly in hard-hit areas such as Calgary, where Genstar was prominent. In the end, Imasco decided to hang on to Genstar Development, which did not upset the subsidiary's management. Frank Thomas, a young Winnipeg engineer who joined Genstar in 1977, had risen to senior management, and applauded the takeover by Imasco, which, he says, represented "a big step up" in ownership. "We survived because no one was interested in buying us. After a while, the folks at Imasco figured, what the heck, we generated cash and they were fond enough of us to keep us."

Thomas came into an Imasco organization that was very much a reflection of Purdy Crawford. While Genstar as a conglomerate seemed to be run for the good of its top executives, at Imasco Thomas saw a focus on people development that other companies lacked. Imasco, he says, "was trying to make the business better by making people better; at [the old] Genstar, the idea was we can make the business better by making head office better." Thomas would thrive, becoming head of the development company and immersed in an Imasco culture that cultivated excellent managers who, in the decades to come, would distinguish themselves elsewhere. It is now legend in Canadian business circles—as it is in the legal community—how Purdy Crawford found bright people, reeled them in, and made them better, and they would always thank Purdy for this, no matter where they ended up.

Purdy felt that, in a conglomerate, the corporate centre, Imasco, had to show it could add value in excess of what the various subsidiaries could achieve on their own. He saw Imasco could earn its keep, and more, through three broad functions: providing financial discipline by working with the unit's managers to set aggressive financial targets; pushing management to develop strategy to meet those targets; and developing superior leaders. On the latter front, Imasco was way ahead of its time.

Thomas, who was still running Genstar Development thirty years later, says that when he does business with other companies he meets people who are talented, but their great flaw is they never worked for Imasco. "My years at Imasco were far more important to me than an MBA." The commitment to management development filtered down and was replicated inside the different subsidiaries. "We soaked it up like a sponge," Thomas says. The development arm put its own management development program in place for every middle manager and up. Each one had a five-year plan, charting what courses they had or had not taken. A senior management program would take executives out of their company for five weeks at, say, a chicken-processing company in North Carolina that was part of Hardee's.

Purdy developed a list of the qualities he looks for in leaders, and it starts with personal integrity, intelligence, self-confidence, and the ability to articulate one's views well and to relate well to people. His best leaders are those who see the big picture, have broad interests, and are open to change. He was an early student of emotional intelligence and of the groundbreaking work of psychologist Daniel Goleman, who showed that people limited to technical skills, or even to cognitive skills, lag far behind in performance those who are also emotionally grounded in self-awareness, self-control, empathy, and social skills. "I found this concept mind opening," Purdy says.

He was more involved in leadership building than just about any other CEO, and the major trait he looked for was that elusive "fire in the belly"—the kind he found in Annette Verschuren, a daughter of Dutch immigrants who farmed in Cape Breton Island. In the 1980s, at age twenty-eight, Verschuren had a good career going in her native Cape Breton, rising to become director of planning for DEVCO, the federal Crown corporation that owned the island's coal mining company. A big day arrived when she had to make a presentation to the board along with DEVCO's CFO and president. The team gave its talk and then took questions, and one of the directors, a heavy-set, round-faced man, started to grill Annette in particular.

Never lacking in confidence, she handled the barrage of questions. She felt an electric current in the air as she dealt with this one director, a guy from central Canada named Purdy Crawford. After the meeting ended and when they were out of earshot, Crawford told her if she were ever interested in leaving DEVCO, he would like her to come see him at Imasco. "She was full of fire and passion, and I was immediately impressed. I said, 'when you are ready to move on, let me know'," Purdy says. "He called me a 'pistol'—he saw that quality in me," recalls Verschuren thirty years later, after a storied career in the retail industry but now sitting in the Toronto boardroom of NRStor, the alternative energy storage company of which she is the chair and CEO. "He saw that I was not laid back—I was proactive and not reactive, and those were the qualities he liked."

74

Verschuren would leave DEVCO, but she did not join Crawford right away. She went to central Canada to join Canada Development Investment Corporation, a federal agency charged with divesting some of Ottawa's collection of industrial holdings. It was work she understood as a former Crown corporation executive. "I didn't believe governments could run business, and so I got to meet the most amazing group of people"—but she yearned to get into operating roles.

Purdy kept an eye on her, then one day called with an offer: would she become Imasco's vice-president of corporate development, a job that required her to be four days on the road and a day back in Toronto? Verschuren resisted because she wanted to avoid being stuck in a staff job—the fate of many women managers—and miss out on operational experience. So she agreed to take the development job for two years, then go into retail—she would later run Imasco's Den for Men and United Cigar Store units. Imasco gave her retail operating experience that she would mine for decades to come.

Verschuren had some rocky moments. Purdy had to hire her over the objections of her immediate superior, who was very old-school. "Basically, I told him to hire her—it was not a very good start." Purdy noted that his young protegée, like many young male executives, sometimes came on strong, and she ruffled feathers at one outside board. "If she had been a man, they would never have thought a second about it," he observes.

In Imasco's Montreal offices, Annette enjoyed the early mornings with Purdy, before the office got humming, when she would sit with him and talk business. He would speak, and she would challenge him. But was he a good CEO? Verschuren admires his ability to develop strong people around him, although he was certainly not a rah-rah type. "He was brilliant at getting the right people in the right spots; his timing was impeccable and he had vision. That's what makes a great CEO."

When Purdy moved on to become non-executive chair in the mid-1990s, Verschuren sensed that it was time for another career change.

She had always yearned to actually run a company, so she left Imasco to manage her own investment vehicle, which became a partner with Michaels, the big US craft and hobby retailer, to bring that concept to Canada. "I was always someone who wanted to be in a leadership position, to manage assets and people and be responsible, and I knew that at a young age." And she would get some opportunities to do that. Later she was recruited by the massive home renovation retailer Home Depot to run its fast-growing subsidiary in Canada, and would later push the Home Depot thrust into China.

But when she left Imasco, Purdy, still chairman, was not happy, and for a short time the two did not talk. In the end, however, he understood that she had to pursue her dream, and they got back to talking. "That is the Maritime connection," she says. "There is something wonderful about that relationship. We have a few bumps along the way and move on."

And it was not just Maritimers. Crawford's ability to spot and develop talent was pervasive in Canadian business. In 1984, just before he joined Imasco, Purdy was the non-university voice on a University of Toronto panel appointed to select a new dean of law to replace Frank Iacobucci, who was moving up to university provost. A young Canadian *wunderkind*, Robert Prichard, was teaching law at Harvard and, at the urging of U of T contacts, threw his name into the ring. Although he was a mere associate professor in his early thirties, the confident, voluble Prichard secured an interview with the panel and gave a strong showing. He knew Crawford only by reputation, but Prichard was told later that, after his persuasive pitch, Purdy joked to other panelists: "I wouldn't mind having that guy sell my law firm." Prichard laughs that the quip sent a kind of mixed message, but it captured his personality. Although there were more seasoned candidates, Prichard was handed the dean's job.

A decade later, in his early forties, he was president of the entire University of Toronto when he got a call that Purdy and Brian Levitt wanted to meet him. This time Purdy made the pitch: would Prichard become an Imasco director? It would be Prichard's first corporate directorship, and he learned a lot. "I got a seminar on how to be a corporate director in a first-class board from the master himself. When you get that Good Housekeeping seal of approval, good things happen." He went onto other top-flight boards, fifteen or so in all, including the roles of chairman of the Bank of Montreal and the Torys law firm, the top executive post at media giant Torstar, and chair of Metrolinx, the public body that coordinates Toronto-area mass transit. "Purdy twice gave me a start," says Prichard, once at the U of T law school and again at Imasco. They are not close friends, but Crawford's role in his life has been huge.

When Purdy left as Imasco's CEO in 1995—while remaining non-executive chairman—he had accomplished a lot. Despite growing skepticism about the effectiveness of conglomerates, Imasco had proved a success for its shareholders, averaging an annual total return of 21 percent over the twenty-nine years from its founding in 1970 to its final year in 1999. At Imasco, there was much Purdy did that was personally and professionally rewarding. When he joined the holding company, his mandate had been to diversify away from tobacco, and he was successful in doing that. But tobacco left a bitter taste in his mouth—the product was increasingly an industrial pariah that operated in a milieu of controversy, with ultra-high taxes and a widespread industry practice of exporting cigarettes and smuggling them back to Canada in the name of higher profits. The illicit export and resmuggling of Canadian tobacco came to make up 20 percent of the Canadian market, and, in the end, anyone remotely linked to the tobacco business was tainted in some way.

In a May 1991 speech, Crawford described the impact of high tobacco taxes and their contribution to the smuggling that tarred the industry. The pattern of ever-increasing taxes meant that the amount of tax paid to buy a package of cigarettes was $4.38 in Windsor,

Ontario, compared with 74 cents across the river in Detroit. He warned that government taxes, on average accounting for about three-quarters of the product's price at retail in Canada, were "deforming virtually every aspect of the tobacco trade. The latest federal and provincial increases are certain to encourage more smuggling; create an even bigger black market; and deprive the government of millions of dollars of lost revenue."

This "deformation" of the market reverberated long after Purdy left Imasco. The company was broken up, and Imperial Tobacco Canada ended up entirely in the hands of BAT. In late July 2008, Imperial announced a settlement with the federal and provincial governments regarding the export of tobacco products to the United States and their resmuggling into Canada. The violations of the *Excise Act* in the late 1980s and early 1990s resulted in a $200 million fine. In addition, a civil agreement required Imperial to pay $50 million in 2008 and a percentage of annual net revenue over fifteen years, adding up to a maximum $350 million.

Imasco was a great experience that allowed Crawford to deploy his management skills on the wider screen of a major Canadian company. But given the turmoil over tobacco, would he do it over again? He admits he is not sure. Yet the Imasco tenure left other legacies—he shaped a cadre of managers who changed Canadian business and helped reconfigure the financial services landscape in a way that benefited Canadian consumers.

# Chapter Six

# BETTING ON ED CLARK

I n 1984, Ed Clark was a man without a job, cut loose from the federal government, where he had worked for over a decade and risen to be one of the most honoured senior civil servants. The word on the street was that he was toxic, having been fired by the new prime minister, Brian Mulroney, to demonstrate to his Progressive Conservative constituency that he would rid the bureaucracy of the statist, anti-business tendencies of the previous Liberal regime.

And Clark had a difficult resumé. He had been a public servant in the true sense of the term—turning policy into action on behalf of his political employers. But he became reviled by much of Canada between the Great Lakes and the Rockies for one of those policies, the National Energy Program (NEP), a dramatic nationalistic overhaul of the oil patch which added further instability to the industry at a time of falling prices and a global recession. He carried the nickname "Red Ed," partly inspired—and totally unwarranted—by his PhD thesis on Tanzanian state socialism. He was blamed for every ill in recession-wracked western Canada and was a hot potato in all of corporate Canada for his allegedly interventionist leanings. But Clark had one big equalizer on his side: Purdy Crawford.

"When I was let go by the government of Canada, the government made clear to people they would not look favourably on my being employed by anyone," says Clark, sitting, almost thirty years later, in the boardroom beside his office, where he is CEO of TD Bank. "That immediately set Purdy in motion, and he called everyone up to say 'This is the smartest guy in Canada, and you would be nuts not to hire him'." That was classic Crawford—he was bucking the wind again. "He gets toughest when the going gets tough. If there is a fight on and a good side and a bad side, he gets right in there," Clark says. Clark agrees that Purdy's backing had a profound impact on his career and, by that measure, a big hand in building Canada Trust—and thus today's TD Bank, which has grown and prospered under Clark's guidance.

The other side of Purdy is that he knows and appreciates talent. As a leader, Clark could see the whole picture, the layers of complexity on any issue, both the broad global panorama and the narrow detail, right down to the trading floor. He knew how markets worked, but he also understood the tension between markets and government, and where both impulses sprang from. He could also be comfortable talking with a human touch to employees. He had been a skilled public servant who carried out the wishes of the government of the day. Yes, he would crack a few heads to get things done, and, yes, he was sometimes unbending, but that was good, too. He would mature, Purdy concluded.

And Crawford has never seen leadership in terms of mutually exclusive compartments—public service versus private company versus professional practice. If people are smart and principled and willing to work very hard, they can succeed just about anywhere. After all, Purdy himself had moved from law to the private sector with a minimum of fuss. And as Clark explained the Dome restructuring, Purdy realized that here was a bureaucrat with a special gift for fashioning clarity out of complexity. Clark is known as someone who, like Purdy, can operate at the same time on different levels—the macro and the micro.

Asked what Crawford saw in him—or in others he has helped—
Clark says it starts with "Are you smart? None of the people he
supports would be slow witted, and he is very smart himself." Purdy,
he says, respects someone who can take him on in an argument and
win. "He has the self-confidence that he doesn't mind losing an
argument—he'd like to lose an argument." And he looks for social
values that align with his, such as never losing sight of your roots and
giving back to the community. "He has done well financially, but that
is not the measure of his success—he is very conscious of doing the
right thing. I believe there is no one associated with Purdy of whom
you would say: 'Oh, I wouldn't invite that person home for dinner'."

Clark grew up in the Toronto suburb of Agincourt in a brainy
household. His father, Samuel Delbert Clark, was a giant in Canadian
sociology and the founding chairman of the sociology department at
the University of Toronto. According to Sinclair Stewart in a profile of
Ed Clark in the *Globe and Mail*'s *ROB Magazine*, "Del Clark studied
social change—political protest, urban poverty and the like—and over
time changed his politics from leftist to Liberal." Clark's mother,
Rosemary, came from an Antigonish, Nova Scotia, family, taught
economics at college, and edited her husband's books. Ed's brother
Samuel also became a sociologist.

Ed completed a BA in economics in 1969 at the University of
Toronto, where he met Brian Levitt, then he enrolled in the master's
program at Harvard and stayed on for his PhD, which involved an
African stint to study the economic strategy of Tanzanian president
Julius Nyerere—and where he worked as an economist in the
Tanzanian government. His thesis, "Socialist Development and Public
Investment in Tanzania," was later circulated in the oil patch, following the implementation of the NEP, as proof of Clark's allegedly
revolutionary leanings. Stewart noted that "[h]e says his critics have
never read the thing. If they had, they'd know it wasn't a socialist
tract, but rather a study of socialism."

According to Stewart, the decision by Clark to steer away from the family's academic path was simple: he thought he would make a terrible academic. His skill, he felt, was in taking something complicated and turning it into something the average individual could grasp. "That's not a particularly good ability for an academic." Instead, Clark joined the Department of Finance in Ottawa as an economist in 1974 and in 1975 took responsibility for parts of the highly controversial Anti-Inflation Board. Clark loved his job, which involved managing 150 people, and he moved quickly up the ladder of the federal public service. He switched over to the Department of Energy, Mines and Resources as assistant deputy minister and was named Canada's civil servant of the year in 1982. He was only thirty-five years old.

But then came the election of 1984, and the Mulroney machine rolled into power. The new Progressive Conservative government was pressured by Alberta cabinet ministers and the Alberta provincial government of Peter Lougheed to make an example out of Ed Clark. But the word went out that Ed was okay in Purdy's book, and ultimately he got hired by Merrill Lynch, the big US investment bank, where he got some valuable grounding in the mergers and acquisitions world. Then, looking for more challenges, he moved over to run Morgan Trust, which was part of Financial Trustco, a financial services empire controlled by the enterprising and mercurial Gerry Pencer. Clark has said he was told by everyone on the Street, including Purdy, that he was out of his mind to work for Pencer and his shaky empire. "I advised him against it," Purdy says in the book by journalist Howard Green, *Banking on America*, which chronicles Clark's career. "But he did it. I was worried that he could get tarnished by the brush of Pencer."

The naysayers were right—Pencer's financial empire would collapse. "That's why I'm running the TD Bank," Clark told Sinclair Stewart. "Because I actually took the completely dumb decision to go to Financial Trustco. Objectively, you've got to admit that was the dumbest decision in the world." Dumb, maybe, but not terminally so. When Financial Trust imploded in the great trust company debacle of the 1980s, Clark was left with a clean-up job, and he did the best he could. He ultimately looked smart as he disposed of the pieces of the trust company, including a chunk sold to Canada Trust. It was generally agreed that Clark made the best deal possible for the public shareholders of Financial Trustco.

Even before he joined Merrill Lynch, he got to know the CEO of Canada Trust, a thoughtful manager named Peter Maurice, who had succeeded the brilliant but belligerent Merv Lahn. There was no job for Clark at the time, but he and Maurice met again when Canada Trust trolled for US savings and loan companies and Merrill Lynch was the investment bank peddling a number of these properties. After the Financial Trustco ordeal and the sale of assets, Maurice made his pitch. Clark's recollection is that Maurice didn't want to be CEO forever and asked if Clark wanted to come over. What's more, Canada Trust was owned by Imasco, with Purdy Crawford at the helm, and, "obviously, when my name came up, [Purdy] was very supportive." Indeed, Ed Clark was "a big Imasco favourite," a former company insider recalls. He became another product of Purdy's willingness to make a bet on people, to find an upstart, an outsider, and capitalize on his or her potential. Ed Clark would keep paying back that bet over and over.

When Clark joined Canada Trust, he says, "the deal with Peter Maurice was [that] I would come over and that 'you tell me when you are ready and I will get out of the way.' It was an easy transition." But it was also a bit of an attitude shift in the executive offices. "I am more hands-on than Peter," Clark admits. "I quickly came to a view of what needed to be done. I do not have a lot of patience to wait till tomorrow, so it was 'let's get on with it'." Canada Trust's momentum had stalled when Clark arrived, and the company suddenly found itself losing market share to the big banks. Clark did some simple things, like getting out of some commercial real estate, pulling back on auto-financing, and pushing investment in branch banking and the brokerage business. He reduced the company's corporate finance risk and reasserted the focus on building the retail brand. It was during his Canada Trust years, according to Sinclair Stewart, "that Clark developed his reputation as a straight-ahead branch-banking operator, proving that he could produce results at a large, publicly traded organization—one competing against the big banks, no less."

All the time, Clark could count on backing from Imasco and Purdy Crawford. Clark saw Crawford as "my owner," and Purdy was on his board of directors. There is often the mistaken impression that Crawford is just a big-picture guy who pays little attention to detail. Instead, "he would be on your back—but in a good way. His job was to make us better than we were," Clark recalls. "What you get is the discipline of having the owner. If you have to go and explain yourself, they [Imasco] had a sensible view that 'I'm not here to pretend I can do banking better than you; otherwise I would fire you.' But you also get the discipline and their willingness to say 'if you need to invest, and it's clearly a sensible thing, I will back it'."

Thanks to Canada Trust, Shoppers, and Imperial Tobacco, Purdy's performance in value creation had been impressive. It was the result of taking a bet on great managers and riding on their skills. But the times were changing. Purdy got airlifted into Imasco because Paul Paré's original in-house succession plan had been scuttled. Now, as he reached his mid-sixties, Purdy had to find someone to succeed him in turn. There was talent in Imasco, but it was not yet ready for the top job.

So Purdy reached back into Osler and plucked Brian Levitt, one of his top acolytes, who in Purdy's absence had continued to add lustre to the firm as a top-rung corporate lawyer. Levitt had been on the Canada Trust and Imasco boards, and as the two men had lunch, Purdy made his pitch: come into Imasco, and if you work out, you are my successor. "I was forty-three and I had a pretty good career, and every lawyer's secret desire is to be a client," Levitt explains. "I had done some big deals and asked myself if I wanted to do it for another twenty years." And after just two years at Imasco, Levitt became Crawford's successor as CEO. Levitt acknowledges this kind of coronation of a friend would not be as simple today—the board would want to be a bigger part of the process. But, he adds, it was a special situation because there was no other natural successor.

Levitt faced a different challenge. The climate had turned against conglomerates as investors looked for more focused companies with a single mandate and more transparent business models. The markets talked of a holding company discount, which meant highly diversified companies were trading below the collective book value of their subsidiaries. For a while, Imasco was in denial. Levitt once told his executives that "the only people in this country who don't think this is a conglomerate are in this room."

Even before he became CEO, Levitt emphasized shareholder relations, making it a priority to get over to London to visit his largest shareholder, BAT, twice a year. By the time he took over in 1995, he had built good links with Martin Broughton, Sir Patrick Sheehy's successor as CEO at BAT. That was vital work because the relationship was changing. When he first came to Imasco, BAT's 42 percent share of the Canadian company had a market value of less than 10 percent of all of BAT. By the end of the 1990s, the companies were valued at about the same, meaning there was huge value locked up in the BAT conglomerate that was not recognized in the share price. And, perversely, a lot of this value was caught up in non-tobacco assets over which it had no control.

BAT had itself become a sprawling entity, extending beyond its tobacco base, beyond Imasco, and into retail and financial services. But it was vulnerable, as was seen in a takeover attempt by the flamboyant raider Sir Jimmy Goldsmith. In the BAT offices in London, there was a new way of thinking: how about scaling back to being a pure player in tobacco?

Levitt began talking to Broughton about how to resolve this imbalance, and the conversation went on for three years. BAT wanted to own all the tobacco business, and the idea arose to do a trade with Imasco's shareholders—to swap the 42 percent of Imasco that BAT owned for all of the Imperial Tobacco business. It was a conversation that would gather force and change the shape of Canadian business.

All this positioning took place against the backdrop of one of the most dramatic periods in Canadian banking. The small club of five major Canadian banks (six, if you count Quebec-concentrated National Bank) was threatening to get a lot smaller. In a shocking series of announcements, Royal Bank and Bank of Montreal announced plans to merge, and Canadian Imperial Bank of Commerce and Toronto Dominion Bank would also join together. That left Bank of Nova Scotia out in the cold, but there was talk of Scotiabank's doing a deal to buy Canada Trust.

The planned mergers sparked an angry outcry from Main Street Canada, and the deals were scuttled in mid-December 1998 by Finance Minister Paul Martin because, he said, they were not in the best interests of Canadians. That left Canada Trust out there as a potential target in a very thin field. Scotiabank and Royal were both candidates to buy the trust company, and CIBC had been kicking tires. But they fell out of the picture as TD Bank, whose philosophical approach to branch banking was similar to Canada Trust's, quickly moved to establish contact with BAT.

On June 8, 1999, stories started flowing out of London that BAT was poised to consolidate its tobacco interests, which meant it would buy all of Imasco, then break it up by selling off all the pieces except Imperial Tobacco of Canada. That meant Shoppers Drug Mart and Canada Trust would be on the selling block. Behind the scenes, negotiations were underway to do this complex unravelling in the most tax-efficient way, with TD Bank's ace negotiator Bill Brock working behind the scenes with BAT in London. Brock remembers BAT's obsession with secrecy—although its officials did feel that Imasco's chair Purdy Crawford was one person they could trust with discretion.

"We on the [Canada Trust] board always saw TD as the real competitor and a bank that understood the Canada Trust model best," says Torrance Wylie. And no one needed a deal more than Charles Baillie, TD's erudite CEO, who knew his bank's relative lack of size and scope, as the smallest of the Big Five, was a challenge. He had already made a daring takeover of Waterhouse, a top-flight US discount stock brokerage, and staked TD's claim to the North American retail investment market. Now he stepped up with an offer to buy Canada Trust. And he was buying more than a trust company. "Charlie Baillie had the incredible courage to say 'we're not buying just a bunch of assets—we are buying a business model and people, and we're going to let that business model take over here and drive us'," Ed Clark says.

Purdy, as chair of the Imasco board, served as all-important liaison between Imasco management and an independent committee of the board. He watched it all unfold, and even as he helped extract a higher share price, he couldn't help feeling some sadness. "It was hard to sell Canada Trust, but it had to be done. I so liked the company." But he also respected TD. He actually had been a director of TD but lasted just two board meetings before Canada Trust came across the bank's radar; he told TD chairman Dick Thomson he would have to resign because of the conflict.

By January 2000, Imasco's shareholders had overwhelmingly accepted BAT's takeover offer. By this time, BAT had already made deals to sell CT Financial, Canada Trust's parent company, and the Shoppers Drug Mart chain. Shoppers went to a New York private-equity group, Kohlberg Kravis Roberts and Co., for $2.55 billion cash, and TD Bank took over CT Financial for $8 billion. Some observers have called it a reverse takeover, arguing that it was not so much a case of TD's taking over Canada Trust but of Canada Trust's taking over much bigger TD. Brian Levitt agrees with that assessment to some degree, but he insists it was a reverse takeover only of the personal banking business, not of the rest of the bank.

Baillie remained TD's CEO for two more years. The race to succeed him was between Ed Clark and Bob Kelly, a first-rate TD banker who hailed from Halifax. On December 20, 2002, Clark won, completing one of the most unlikely journeys in Canadian business, from star policy-maker in Ottawa to a pariah of Canadian business to the top of one of Canada's elite banks. (Kelly left TD but surfaced as a chief executive in the US banking industry.)

And there was the element of a reverse takeover, as Ed Clark and his team unleashed people throughout the TD organization who spread the Canada Trust model that the bank would embrace for the future. Then, Clark took TD to the United States in a series of acquisitions, a transformation that propelled the institution from perennial number five to a strong number two among Canada's banks. In late 2013, Clark was looking at another year in the job before handing it over to his successor, Bharat Masrani.

As Clark prepared to leave, the jury was still out on some of those expansion moves, but no one disputes that Ed Clark has changed the look of banking in North America. Under his leadership, TD has seen remarkable growth. From 2006 to 2013, it went from having no retail operations in the United States to 1,300 branches; by whatever measure you use, it is one of the top dozen largest banking networks in the United States. Overall, its assets have tripled during Clark's tenure to $835 billion, and it has gone from a $76 million loss the year Clark took over to an impressive string of profitability.

How important has Purdy Crawford been to the success of Clark and TD? He is not a banker, but he is a banker of talent. He sees someone with fire in the belly, and he puts the name away for safekeeping, a deposit on the future. He has done that with Ed Clark and Brian Levitt, with Annette Verschuren and Deborah Alexander. He backed the hiring of Clark at Canada Trust, supported his re-energization of the trust company, and picked Brian Levitt as his Imasco successor. Levitt was in charge of Imasco when it was sold to TD. The Crawford-Clark-Levitt triumvirate laid the foundation for the modern TD and, as Clark was leaving the bank in 2014, Levitt was filling the role of the bank's chairman.

Financial history is often written as a maelstrom of great forces, of recession, depression, and business cycles, but it is always, at the core, about people and how they interact. Ed Clark says he is one of a lot of people who have ended up with great careers because of Purdy Crawford. "It is his intuitive feel for potential and a willingness to take chances with people and not be going with the crowd. If people are anti-somebody, he doesn't care. He has his own view of value and he just follows it. If you are in a knife fight, that is the guy you want in the corner. There are a lot of people who are very nice and honourable until the going gets rough. They don't want to be there because it might hurt their reputation, but Purdy is there."

The knife fights would happen again and again, and the stakes would be high.

# Chapter Seven

# ELDER STATESMAN

L ean, athletic, ultra-confident, Paul Tellier is one of Canada's executive superstars, a hard-charging dynamo who rose to head Canada's public service, privatize one of its iconic companies—Canadian National Railway—and led it through a transformation that made it one of the continent's best railways. He is also another who studied at the feet of Purdy Crawford, who, as a director of CN, became a valued advisor to Tellier, a man just eight years younger.

According to Tellier, one of Purdy's greatest gifts was the art of the second look—being able to sit on a decision overnight and take another clear-headed view of it. "I tend to be very aggressive and very intense," acknowledges Tellier, now a busy professional director. "I basically come across pretty hard, [saying] 'What the hell are we doing in this company?'" But then he stops and reminds himself of Purdy Crawford's words. When Tellier was running CN, Crawford, as a trusted director, would say, "Paul, why don't you sleep on it?" Tellier says that "only a fool would ignore that. You regroup with your team and ask, 'is there something we are ignoring? Why is Crawford asking this?'" Then Tellier would go around the room and canvas his managers. They might still go down the route they had chosen originally, but the decision would now have been thought through with all its repercussions.

Tellier's education epitomized the new role of Purdy Crawford. When he retired as CEO of Imasco and handed the torch to Brian Levitt, Purdy moved back to Toronto and became non-executive chairman of the company. He and Bea moved into a rented condominium in the upscale midtown area around the corner of Yonge and St. Clair—they liked the building so much they later bought a unit. Then, when Imasco was broken up, the chairman's role vaporized. But Purdy still had two office locations where he could hang his hat: he was chair of AT&T Canada, a troubled telecommunications firm, and he was invited back to Osler as counsel to the law firm—not a senior partner, but more of an advisor. He hired a new executive assistant, Sue Lucas, who became not just an employee, but also a confidante and advisor. She remembers that he pondered his choice of offices before finally saying "Osler's it is." It was like coming home.

It was from his Osler office that he embarked on his late-career roles as legal *éminence grise*, corporate governance guru, and Canada's most respected corporate director and pre-eminent mentor. He was no longer a lawyer or an executive, but a brand. "Purdy Crawford" meant experience, networking, teamwork, a lack of overpowering ego, but also toughness and persistence. He could get the big jobs done, and he could influence the texture of Canadian business more than anyone else just by weaving his subtle webs of contacts and service.

Beyond Imasco, CN was his great triumph in directorship, and once again Purdy Crawford was at the centre of a defining moment in Canadian business. CN has a storied history, having been a federal government assembly of troubled railways in the early twentieth century. By the 1990s, it was very much a creature of government—a Crown corporation with a top-heavy bureaucracy. Then, in 1992, Brian Mulroney's Progressive Conservative government got into privatization mode and installed the can-do Energizer bunny Paul Tellier as CN's CEO.

Tellier, then fifty-two, was a creature of bureaucracy, but his ultimate legacy was to overcome bureaucracy. Born in Joliette, Quebec, he was educated at Université Laval and got a law degree from Oxford before going to Ottawa in the 1970s and rising through the ranks of the federal public service. He became the country's top civil servant in August 1985 when Muloney appointed him clerk of the Privy Council. Seven years later, when he moved over to CN, he was accompanied by Michael Sabia, a bright young bureaucrat who was one of the architects of the controversial but successful revenue-generating goods and services tax. Sabia would be Tellier's right-hand man and chief financial officer.

In 1993, as CN readied itself for privatization, the government changed with the Liberal win in that year's federal election. Tellier switched political masters, but his mandate did not change. The new transport minister, Doug Young, huddled with Tellier on how to proceed with privatization. Tellier recalls that Young asked what the government could do to make the exercise a success. The answer: get a good board. "I don't give a damn whether directors are Conservative, NDP, or Liberal, but make sure they have something to contribute," Tellier told him. Young delivered, and at the top of his list was Purdy Crawford.

"He was probably one of the best corporate directors I have come across," Tellier says, a status he attributes to three major attributes. First, he does his homework and arrives well prepared. Second, he understands that the job of a director is not to tell management how to manage the place. The proper role is to ask if management has the right people and knows where it is going. The fashionable word is "strategy," but essentially it is a question of where are you now and where you want to be in five years. And third, that reflective side. Purdy would never say, as some directors do, "don't do this." "He would say, 'Paul, when you get back to your office, you might want to just think about it for a few days.' He would not dictate his views or impose his opinion. It was a great quality on the part of a director."

For Tellier, who operated in a very political atmosphere, it was valuable that Purdy was adept in making sure directors did not cross the line and get involved in the company. CN had some good directors, but, as a Crown corporation in transition, it was saddled with political appointees who didn't have much to contribute in strategy but had ideas on how the railway could serve political ends. "He was very good at reminding his colleagues on the board: don't get into this, leave it to management," Tellier says. And he would be a rock in providing advice during the privatization—such as under-promise but over-deliver.

Tullio Cedraschi, the veteran investment manager who ran the CN pension fund, says the strength of a director is often his ability to rein in a smart but impatient CEO. "That's where the genius of Purdy comes in—to be able to handle a horse that is kicking up a little dust as he prepares for the race." In fact, Crawford was part of a transfusion of private sector directors who helped advise Tellier and Sabia, both of whom were top-flight bureaucrats who could navigate government but novices at business. Other key appointees were Cedric Ritchie, chairman of Bank of Nova Scotia—another Maritimer who had scrambled to the top of the Bay Street pole—and Ray Cyr, former president of Bell Canada. Another addition was Maureen Kempston Darkes, who had gone from Osler lawyer to the top of General Motors of Canada. Others would join, such as Jim Gray, a veteran oilman from Calgary who became a friend and key collaborator. Purdy, Gray says, "has a very subtle way, and when he has made up his mind—and he is usually right—he has a wonderful way of controlling a conversation. He is open to new ideas and not stubborn but has a sense of where he wants to get to." That was valuable at CN in a time of change. "The initial public offering at CN was a defining moment in Canada, and he was a central figure in that activity."

As with Osler and Imasco, Crawford knew the key to CN's future was talent development. He assumed a critical role as chairman of the board's human resources committee, which drew on his interest in leadership and on his understanding of the way companies work. Purdy always pondered how directors could influence a company's culture in a way that helped drive its growth. A director cannot manage but, by monitoring strategy and building a leadership culture, can help create a framework for management to do its job. In this way Purdy, who often seemed like a very traditional businessman, again was ahead of every one else.

Crawford worked closely with CN's top human resources people to develop and review incentive programs so that they were serving the right purpose in the long run, not just for the next quarter. "He taught me a lot about getting the right person and promoting younger people," Tellier says. Even though both men have long since left CN, "a few times a year, he drops me a note to say, 'Paul, you should see so and so!'—either someone to pick my brain or it's a guy I should know."

The CN privatization was a nail biter. Directors remember assembling for a critical meeting on the eve of the Quebec referendum on October 30, 1995, knowing a vote for sovereignty could scuttle the railway's public offering. The board watched by television as the votes came in and the pro-Canada forces won by a whisker. Ottawa sold all its shares to investors in a blockbuster initial public offering that poured $2.6 billion into the federal government's coffers.

And Tellier was far from done. He knew CN needed efficiency—and a dramatic paring of the company's bloated cost structure—but also scale and stretch. He made a number of sorties aimed at merging with parts or all of Canadian Pacific, the other national rail carrier, but was rebuffed. Then he became consumed with the dream of building a north-south transportation network to draw on Canada's ever tightening free trade relationship with first the United States, and later, Mexico. In 1998, Tellier made the big move in that direction by buying storied Illinois Central, which saw CN expand its focus from its exclusively east-west orientation into a north-south ribbon of moving goods.

It was an important acquisition in other ways, for it allowed Tellier to push ahead to make CN a rigorously operated freight railway that delivered with on-time scheduling and service. That transition got a big boost from promoting former Illinois Central president Hunter Harrison to a key vice-president's position at CN. In a sense, the Illinois Central deal was about more than getting a railway—it was buying the best operational talent in the industry in Harrison, a tough-as-nails railwayman out of Memphis. Harrison had achieved a remarkable turnaround at Illinois Central—like CN, a fabled railway that had lost its way.

It is surprising how often talent is the crucial ingredient in mega-mergers—the chance to buy a great manager or slate of managers in order to absorb their expertise, and hope you don't lose them in the transition. TD did that when it bought Canada Trust, whose assets included Ed Clark and his personal banking team. Purdy Crawford supported that move then, and again in CN's case, as he understood that Hunter Harrison was the best operator in the industry.

Harrison brought to CN the formula he had used to turn around Illinois Central. At CN, they called it "precision railroading," at the heart of which lay the fundamental principle that the trains must run on time. As Reuters described it in a 2012 article, "[t]raditionally, railways had played fast and loose with schedules, holding trains until they were hauling as much cargo as possible. From the perspective of single trains, flexibility can seem efficient, but that misses the big picture. Locomotives don't get where they are needed; crews are idle; cargo is late." Under Harrison, CN started moving assets more quickly and shipping more cargo using less equipment. Instead of waiting to fill a train, it focused on moving shipments to their destination on time. It cracked down on shifts that traditionally started late and ended early, and instituted an unrelenting regime of cost paring.

A key measure of railway efficiency is operating ratio, which measures operating costs as a percentage of revenue—the lower the better. When Harrison arrived in 1998, CN's operating ratio was 75.1. By the time he became CEO in 2003, the ratio had fallen to 69.8, and for several years before the financial crisis hit in 2008, it came in below 65. Rival Canadian Pacific's ratio lagged far behind, and, in fact, CN became known as North America's best railway.

Purdy, as the CN board's human resources champion, was heavily immersed in all these changes. Ed Lumley, a former federal cabinet minister and long-serving vice-chair with investment bank BMO Nesbitt Burns, was involved in the initial public offering and later became a CN director. He recalls of Purdy: "We all knew the guy had a brilliant mind and he showed great leadership." One indication of this regard was the extent to which CN would dip into Purdy's talent pool.

Crawford was still chair at Imasco when Tellier called one day to say that he had hired Claude Mongeau, one of Imasco's managerial prospects, as his chief financial officer. "I took a gulp and said 'you are lucky—he is incredibly good and it's a better job for him'." Mongeau would thrive at CN under both Tellier and Harrison, and is now CN's CEO. And Mongeau's chief financial officer is Luc Jobin, another Imasco alumnus. "Purdy had the innate ability to pick young bright people," Lumley says, "If you look at key people at CN today, they were employed by Purdy."

One of the challenges was getting Tellier and Harrison, both big personalities, to work together. They had complementary skills—Tellier was good in handling government and was very big-picture, while Harrison was the ultimate operator, and they both had healthy egos. Yet the collaboration worked. After Illinois Central was absorbed into the CN network, the duo followed up with another big expansion try—an overture to merge with BNSF, the giant US transcontinental carrier, but Washington shot down the bid.

CN chairman David McLean, a Vancouver real estate entrepreneur who headed the CN board from 1994 to his retirement in spring 2014, saw the failed BNSF bid as a turning point for Tellier. "We had just gone through the BNSF thing and got shut down by the US. Paul is always looking for mountains to climb and there were not a lot of mountains left at CN." The company would add the Wisconsin Central line, giving it even wider coverage in the United States, but a lot of the building blocks were in place for Tellier's continental dream.

As Tellier got into his sixties, he was looking at career options. According to Purdy, the CEO didn't want to leave CN, which he had dragged out of the federal government's clutches, but he understood that Harrison should now run the company. He could not move up to chairman of the board—McLean, the son of a career CN employee, was entrenched in that role. As well, Tellier wanted to stay in Montreal. Then, the CEO's job at Bombardier came into his sights.

Bombardier is a pillar of the Montreal corporate establishment, having risen from its roots as a rural maker of snowmobiles to become a diversified transportation giant, with interests not just in leisure craft for snow and water, but also in rail and commuter jets. But the company and its ruling family—descendants of snowmobile pioneer Joseph-Armand Bombardier—needed a skilled CEO as it faced big challenges in their key commuter jet business. Its fortunes had plummeted after the 9/11 terrorist attacks sent the global air travel industry into a downward spiral. Joseph-Armand's son-in-law, the company's great builder, Laurent Beaudoin, was stepping into the background. There was also the growing impression that, as a result of governance standards accompanying its New York Stock Exchange listing, the company would move away from the tight family control of the past.

Purdy regrets now that he did not urge Tellier to approach with more caution. He knows families do not give up control easily. "If I had thought about it, I would have told him it wouldn't have turned out that way—they wouldn't be out of it at all. I blame myself for not questioning Paul. I regret not being blunter with him," Purdy says. And yet a savvy Tellier no doubt knew the perils—another very capable non-family manager had been eased out of the company's top job.

David McLean had no idea of the drama unfolding when he flew into Toronto one evening in January 2003 for a round of CN board meetings. He was slated to head over to Purdy's office in the morning for a session of the human resources committee. As he arrived, he was told that Crawford and Tellier were waiting for him—and right away, he could sense the landscape shifting. Tellier was leaving, and McLean had to consult the board. "I have to make sure it happens right," he told Tellier. "You are the father of CN, and when the father walks out the door, things happen." The human resources meeting unfolded, and it became obvious the next CEO would be Harrison—indeed, the board elected him unanimously. Then McLean had to choreograph a joint announcement with Bombardier and worried about how the market would react. But the Street knew Hunter Harrison was a good operator, nobody panicked, and the stock dipped slightly, then moved up again.

Paul Tellier went to Bombardier, but, as Purdy worried might occur, he was gone in less than two years after a dispute over strategy with the Bombardier family, which retrenched its control over the firm.

Hunter Harrison, meanwhile, settled easily into his new role at CN, and continued the transformation of the company that he and Tellier had begun. He had a great run at CN and, at the end of 2009 when his contract wound up, retired to occupy himself in horse-farming interests in Connecticut and Florida. With Harrison's exit, Claude Mongeau took over as CEO, finally assuming the job for which he had been groomed after leaving Imasco, and Luc Jobin became CFO. "It is amazing how it all comes around," says David McLean. "They are all Purdy disciples. Purdy is not afraid to pick up the phone and encourage someone. Others will think about it and not do it, but he does it."

After the CN transformation, a lot of the Canadian public's attention concerning railways shifted to its rival, iconic nation-building Canadian Pacific, which had not kept pace with CN in making necessary changes in efficiency. CP also ran smack-dab into a new breed of activist investors who had no patience with underperforming boards and management. In 2011 and 2012, hedge fund investor Bill Ackman led an assault on CP, its board, and CEO Fred Green. His candidate to replace Green: master railwayman Hunter Harrison. Ackman won his proxy battle, engineered an overhaul of the CP board, and Harrison roared out of retirement to take command in an effort to replicate the changes he had made at CN. In the midst of this whirlwind makeover of CP, Harrison could look back warmly on Crawford's role on the CN board. "He was the most senior director, probably the most well respected guy on the board, and he had a lot of influence. If the CEO would convince Purdy of something, that was the way to go—it swung a lot of votes. He had all the right stuff."

Over the years, that right stuff has given Purdy a reputation for being a thoughtful director. He has often been called on to give his views on governance, particularly in the late 1990s and early 2000s, when boards were asleep at the switch at companies such as Enron and WorldCom, resulting in catastrophic scandals. The scandals led to a wave of governance legislation in the United States, which washed into Canadian boardrooms. One repercussion was a new emphasis on "box ticking"—measuring and comparing boards' processes on everything from diversity to director independence. Crawford welcomed this trend to accountability, although he feels that strict adherence to the rules is not enough—even boards that perform well in the box ticking can be totally dysfunctional. Directors have to exhibit a basic integrity, good judgment, and common sense. And good directors have to be more than qualified in their official credentials—they have to be able to step through the minefields of personalities and the politics of boards.

Tullio Cedraschi, now retired from the role of CN pension chief, believes that in the post-Enron atmosphere there is excessive reliance on the science of corporate governance, with endless measurement of factors such as directors' independence, board risk management, succession planning—the list goes on. Cedraschi's prescription is simpler: "If you get a Purdy Crawford on the board, you are getting good governance." Certainly, sound processes and measurement can improve things, but at the core, it is about personality. "How do you evaluate judgment and critical interventions, and the mentoring of executives, including high-ego CEOs? Judgment and ethics are difficult to define but you know them when you see them. It is a little like beauty—you know a Purdy when you see one." And good directors become self-perpetuating, creating board cultures that last long after individuals have come and gone. That is what happened at CN. "Good people select good people, and bad people select less good people.... If you hire a Purdy Crawford, he probably has some feeling for people who resemble him," Cedraschi says.

For Crawford himself, one of the biggest challenges over his boardroom career was facing the reality that the CEO might not be the right person for the job. In those cases, the board has to lead the way in easing out that person and hiring someone else. Many corporate coups are not solely the product of aggressive activist investors but can be traced to inactive or derelict boards, and hedge fund investors simply jump on the opportunity such boards create. Even though directors might agree with the external criticism of the CEO, "they get comfortable and don't want to rock the boat," Purdy says.

He encountered at least one situation where the board, in its written assessment, had given a CEO high praise. But Purdy and another director privately knew this was not the right person, even though they found him personally compelling in manner and education. The problem is that directors pull their punches when they do written assessments, but when they sit down in a private get-together, they are more frank. Purdy believes that in-camera directors' meetings, which have become a regular feature of board activities over the past decade, are highly beneficial. Without the CEO in attendance, directors can let down their hair and conduct a realistic assessment of the company's top manager. In this case, the CEO did leave the company, and Purdy believes the man was actually relieved. He knew he was not measuring up.

Crawford's skills would be called on time and again with his other major board appointment, AT&T Canada, of which he became chairman in 2002. If CN was a triumphant experience, AT&T was a mess, and it took all of Purdy's skills to turn it into, if not a triumph, at least a less-bad outcome. Practising the art of the possible became his hallmark as a director and as a crisis manager, which he demonstrated in spades during the asset-backed commercial paper crisis.

AT&T Canada was the product of shaky public policy and bad strategic decisions. It was the successor to CNCP Communications, a pioneering joint venture of the two railway companies that bound the nation together in a telegraph system in the early decades of the twentieth century. CNCP became Unitel, which became controlled by Ted Rogers's Rogers Communications and emerged as the vehicle to take on Bell in the long-distance telephone market. That attempt largely failed, and the remnants were acquired by US telecom giant AT&T. The idea was to bind together the new breed of local communications suppliers in a national network to take on the big three providers— Bell, Rogers, and Telus. AT&T invested heavily, including $2.4 billion in a merger with Metronet, the largest of Canada's local phone hookups. The US parent piled billions of dollars of debt onto the Canadian subsidiary's balance sheet, and the company was draining money.

Crawford heard from an old Imasco colleague named Dan Somers, who was now the chief financial officer of New York-based AT&T. Would he take on the role of chairman of its Canadian arm? Purdy agreed, but when he got into the company, he recalls being "flabbergasted" at how poorly it was run. He helped AT&T Canada recruit an experienced telecom executive, John McLennan, a former Bell Canada president, to run the business. As vice-chair and CEO, McLennan had no illusions about this salvage job: "AT&T Canada was the biggest dog in the country—it was terrible."

Yet another Maritimer, born and raised in Cape Breton, McLennan left home on a hockey scholarship to Clarkson College in upstate New York, picked up a couple of degrees, and rose to the top of the telecom business. But by the time AT&T contacted hm, he had slipped into quasi-retirement at his home on the Atlantic near beautiful Mahone Bay in Nova Scotia. Despite the dire state of its Canadian assets, he could see possibilities. "Sometimes, in the muck, there is great opportunity," McLennan says. He formed an alliance with fellow Nova Scotian Purdy Crawford as they tried to cope with AT&T Canada's star-crossed business and its nearly $5 billion in debt. McLennan renewed the management team by hiring John MacDonald—an old colleague at Bell and a fellow Maritimer—as well as chief financial officer David Lazzarato, a veteran executive in the communications industry. But it needed Purdy's strength at the board level.

McLennan travelled down to New York to talk to parent AT&T about the next move. The telecom giant said it would pay out the Canadian firm's shareholders, but it was not prepared to address the $5 billion in debt. McLennan remembers how Crawford broke the news to AT&T Canada's board that its parent was cutting it loose. The essence of Purdy's message: "This will be a rough ride, and if any of you don't want to go through it, that's okay—there is no shame in that. But I'm sticking with the management team, and we will take this company through a restructuring. Who knows what will come out the other side?" Then he put it to the board that "I'm in, and who else is in?" McLennan says that, when Purdy looked around the room, "of course, everybody's in."

Thus began the jousting with hostile US bondholders, who often questioned the credibility of this Canadian lawyer. Purdy insisted he was the best friend they had. Ultimately, they came to their senses, and exchanged their debt for 90 percent of the equity of the company, clearing the way for a reorganized AT&T Canada to recover.

The experience exposed a rarely seen side of Purdy Crawford. At a board meeting one evening in Toronto, Purdy lost it. The target of his wrath was a shareholder who was being obstreperous. McLennan recalls that Purdy raised his voice and told the man he was being very unreasonable. His message was: "I've been in this game a long time and I get along well with people, and I don't get along with you." There was palpable tension in the room until it was broken by a phone call—some people were joining the meeting through a conference call. It demonstrated the passion that Crawford carried into the process, because this was a company that needed to be saved.

And they did save it. With the parent out of the picture, AT&T Canada, now in bankruptcy protection, rebranded itself as Allstream and began to rebuild its business. It came out of protection in 2002, was valued at $450 million, and was sold eleven months later to Manitoba Telephone Systems for $1.75 billion. "It worked out not badly," McLennan says, adding that "you get very close to individuals during these intense times. What I truly respect about Purdy is his calm quiet leadership, always focused on the right issue and directing meetings toward the right conclusion." And he was on the receiving end of the famous Crawford method of resolving issues. Purdy would phone up and say something like, "John, I listened to what you said, and have you ever thought of this?" It was not hectoring, but gentle, persistent guidance—the strongest kind of leadership, McLennan says.

A decade later, David Lazzarato, now a professional director and media consultant, would remember Purdy as "the master of the soft skills"—those often intangible but valuable leadership attributes, such as listening, communication, persuasion, and networking.

Lazzarato, who is also chair of the board of governors at McMaster University, says Purdy never fell into the common trap of leaders who explicitly try to deploy soft skills. "I never got the sense time was being sacrificed by Purdy. He could drive a time line and use the soft skills at the same time."

Crawford admits the AT&T Canada period was one of the few times he wore his frustration on his sleeve, but it worked out. It also added another useful contact to his bulging Rolodex. He got to know Steve Halperin, a corporate lawyer with the Goodmans law firm who sat on the AT&T Canada board as a representative of his client, British Telecom. "Those were tough times, and there developed a bunker mentality with fellow directors," Halperin says. A few years later, the two men would be thrown together again—this time with Canada's financial system hanging in the balance.

Increasingly, companies with challenges, big and small, were recognizing the value of Crawford's blend of toughness and persuasiveness. He became the go-to director for a number of companies, including Petro-Canada and Maritime family businesses such as those owned by Ganongs, Braggs, and McCains. But Purdy was about more than being in the trenches. He also thought deeply about how those trenches should be constructed in terms of regulatory and legislative sandbags.

He became identified with two of the most important waves of the late twentieth and early twenty-first centuries: the emphasis on good corporate governance and the need for more effective securities regulation. With his background, he was perfect for the task. He renewed his role as the natural centrepiece for key panels to decide the future of Canada's capital markets, a calling he had earned in 1965 with the Kimber Committee. And just as the Kimber Committee worked against the backdrop of Windfall and the scandalous stock promotions of its era, Purdy's new activism was also rooted in scandal. The late 1990s was a time of egregious lapses in the oversight of corporate directors, as captured by the Enron and WorldCom debacles in the

United States and the collapse of Arthur Andersen, a once-formidable auditing firm. The outcry over a broken governance system pulled Crawford back into the fray.

One his first forays was entering the debate about investment analysts and their role in securities markets. The analysts whose buy-sell calls move markets often work for investment banks, which sell the securities of the firms the analysts cover. This mix of relationships became glaring in the go-go era of the dot-com bubble. To sort out this potential conflict, Crawford chaired an Ontario Securities Commission (OSC) group looking into analysts' standards. The blue-chip group included some of the country's corporate titans but also a former mining geologist named Maureen Jensen, who was now an official at the Toronto Stock Exchange. She would become a close friend and another of his mentoring subjects. The group reported in October 2001, with recommendations on how analysts could retain independence in the face of conflicts.

Then Crawford dove into the Securities Act, the legislation he had originally co-drafted back in the 1960s. He headed a five-year review advisory committee to comb through the legislation and propose updates. The review committee's first recommendation to the Ontario government was something Crawford had urged for decades: the need for a single, coordinated approach to securities regulation in Canada. "It is our very strong view that a nation that commands only two percent of the global economy suffers daily from a regulatory regime which is comprised of 13 separate regulators," the report warned.

As he drove the committee to complete its report, he lent the inimitable Purdy touch to the proceedings. Susan Wolburgh Jenah sat on the committee in her role as general counsel and a director of the OSC. Purdy was an effective chair, she says, because he kept the committee moving. "He had this knack for cutting through to the heart of an issue and letting you know when it was time to move on; you knew when there was enough said."

And yet, she adds, he had an inclusive way: "Even if he thought he knew the right answer, he didn't always disclose it. He wanted everyone to say his or her bit." Wolburgh Jenah was truly impressed with how much interest he had in people, no matter how high or lowly. "I would invite members of my team at the OSC to meetings. He never made them feel like second tier or second string; he would always ask questions about their background. You can't fake that, right?"

The securities law review also allowed free expression for one of Purdy's little habits: sending clippings about things that would matter to the people he worked with and cared about. Osler's securities lawyer Janet Salter was the key staff lawyer for the committee, and she became Purdy's link to other members of the committee. She would distribute the clippings, often annotated with Purdy's comments and underlining. As Osler lawyers began asking to be included, he expanded the format into stapled bundles of articles that Salter, working with Sue Lucas, would put together with the title "Purdy's Picks." It circulated through Osler's legal team and then to selected people on the outside. In time, it would grow to a circulation of between 250 and 300. Had he sold advertising, the articles would have made a mint, because they were seen by the people who mattered in Canadian business.

"Purdy's Picks" suggest a restless, far-ranging mind at work. They might, in a single issue, offer a *Harvard Business Review* piece on boardroom dysfunction and a David Brooks column on immigration from the *New York Times*. And the genesis of "Purdy's Picks" actually went all the way back to Imasco. One of the companies in the conglomerate's stable owned a jet in which Purdy occasionally would ride. As he looked around for something to read, he was aghast to discover that the primary material on board consisted of girlie magazines. These high fliers had two hours' free time on a plane and this is what they read? He replaced them with business magazines. "He became very adamant that people should be very knowledgeable about the business side—and not just business but political happenings impacting the world or your world view," Salter says.

"It is what 'Purdy's Picks' is all about—not about drafting a stock option plan but how to understand the bigger regulatory and public policy issues around any particular matter. And it goes much broader than that—political, social, environmental, diversity, anything like that. He is open to other people submitting things and he will give them credit." In the Osler firm, he felt everyone should have access to the Picks—that it was part of one's personal development as a business lawyer.

How did he have time to pick his picks? He was still getting up early and tried to get in some reading before he left for the office. Besides *Forbes*, *Fortune*, and other magazines, he would devour anything by US historian Doris Kearns Goodwin, either her study of Lincoln's cabinet, *Team of Rivals*, or later, her detailed examination of the Theodore Roosevelt–William Howard Taft era, a book called *Bully Pulpit*.

And he could make seemingly improbable connections in his recommendations of reading material. Chris Huskilson, a young engineer, was trying to build Emera, the Nova Scotia power company, as a private business, having sprung from a former provincial Crown corporation. Purdy pointed him the direction of the biography of Citigroup builder Sandy Weill. It might have been another industry, another time, but it was a study in company building. If Crawford's tastes tend to run a bit toward US or international leaders, it just reflects the volume of work available. The two-volume life of John A. Macdonald by Richard Gwyn is "pretty damn good—he was as good a leader as any of the Founding Fathers," Purdy insists.

Back in Toronto from Montreal, he and Bea were comfortable in their midtown condo. It became a focal point for a Crawford brood which swelled to six children and seventeen grandchildren and a posse of visiting cousins and in-laws. This next generation would visualize Purdy as holding a book in his hand and often reading to them.

They would go over and say, "Grandpa! Book!" And so he became known as "Grandpa Book."

He spent more time at home, but not a lot more. Perhaps his biggest advisory gig was the Crawford Panel, the short-form moniker for an Ontario government commission on the underpinnings of a single Canadian securities regulator. Again, he was surrounded by esteemed panelists, including Jacques Ménard, BMO Nesbitt Burns's Quebec chief; Claude Lamoureux, head of the powerful Ontario Teachers' Pension Plan; and John MacNaughton, a respected former investment banker and pension fund director. But he also reached out to people he knew would gain immensely from the experience.

Legal scholar Dawn Russell got to know Purdy when she was the holder of the Purdy Crawford Chair in Business Law at Dalhousie. When she served as dean of the law school, he was a key advisor and benefactor. As with so many others, Crawford kept close tabs on Russell. "When I finished being dean in 2005, Purdy called to say 'what are you thinking about?' He asked me to be on the Crawford Panel, which was a tremendous learning opportunity for me."

Purdy feels the panel's final report, released on July 6, 2006, is the most comprehensive expression of his own research and thinking—a study in the Canadian brand of co-operative federalism, or the art of the possible applied to government process. The challenge, as the report describes it, is that "Canada is the only major country in the world without a single securities regulator. As well, there is profound concern about ineffective enforcement of securities regulation—a domestic and international embarrassment for Canada."

The problem is the politics of Confederation. Regionally focused provincial politicians block every attempt at reform. Hence, the report is a careful balancing of the need for a single regulatory voice and a governance system that reflects regional diversity. According to Dawn Russell, the panel's great breakthrough was to get Ontario to sign on to the one-jurisdiction, one-vote model. The Crawford report stipulates that the governing body should be "[a] Council of Ministers with political accountability to the Canadian public in their respective jurisdictions." Each jurisdiction would have one vote in the selection of the board and the system's key adjudicators, as well as in the adoption of rules.

By getting Ontario to agree to this model, despite the province's overweighting in securities trading, the panel seemed to break the logjam that had blocked reform. Yet, there was no immediate movement on the issue. The initiative floated back up to the federal level and to a centralized approach that some provinces, such as Quebec and Alberta, would never accept. It was a missed opportunity, says Dawn Russell, who is now president of Saint Thomas University in Fredericton. In an interview in late 2013, she noted that she kept running into people involved in the campaign for a single regulator. "We are looking back longingly at the Crawford report and wondering why we didn't jump at it. I got to see how hard Purdy worked and how deeply he cared about what was good for Canada."

In a new proposal which surfaced in 2013, Ontario, British Columbia, and Ottawa agreed to a single regulator and hoped others would join, but it is still unlikely that all the dissidents will fall into line. Still, the new plan reflects some of Purdy's political pragmatism and a respect for provincial jurisdictions and co-operative federalism.

Frank McKenna has watched this evolution both as premier of New Brunswick and now as a bank executive. Any kind of national initiative that involves a compromise on provincial powers is "never an easy job—this is herding cats." Purdy, he says, did not hit a grand slam, "but he moved the runners around." McKenna says the Crawford Panel helped to air the issue and allowed people to become sensitized to the debate. "Sometimes public policy has to set a while and ferment." It is, he says, "a typical Canadian problem, a typical Canadian approach, and it will get there piecemeal. It will end up getting done." The Crawford Panel, he predicts, will be hailed as a major step toward that destination.

## Chapter Eight

# CANADA'S MENTOR

I t is a Monday night in late October 2013 at Toronto's Fairmont Royal York Hotel, and seven hundred of Canada's business leaders—including a powerful contingent of females—are attending the glittering gala hosted by Catalyst, the advocacy group to advance women in corporations. Catalyst holds this dinner annually to honour its champions in the business community, and tonight's award winners are impressive. They include Lorraine Mitchelmore, the Newfoundlander who heads Shell Canada, and Colleen Johnston, the chief financial officer of TD Bank. One individual is being given special recognition for his lifetime contribution: Purdy Crawford, who, in the words of Catalyst international president (and fellow Nova Scotian) Deborah Gillis, "was instrumental in building a pipeline of women ready to serve in Canada's boardrooms."

Purdy is there, but he does not speak. He does not have to—it is a Purdy Crawford love-in. In her witty speech, Alex Johnston, Catalyst Canada's executive director—and daughter of the governor general—paints a picture of the condescending advice doled out to women in the 1950s by popular self-help books. Among the lamentable suggestions: wives must be good cooks to keep the breadwinner happy; they should not speak unnecessarily as if to nag; and when the marriage goes on the rocks, it is time to bring out the frilly underwear.

Around the time women were urged to purchase frilly underwear, she says, Purdy began his work in championing women, including Bertha Wilson, who, with Purdy's support, rose from a minor support role to become first female Supreme Court justice. As we have seen, he identified, early in their careers, the talents of women such as Annette Verschuren and Deborah Alexander. "He was instrumental in making sure they got the opportunities to gain experience which led to senior roles and corporate board service, and they in turn have been champions of other women, helping to grow the pipelines," Johnston says.

In a video, Crawford, in his unassuming style, tries to describe what happened. He feels that part of his role in heading high-profile commissions was a chance to develop talent—to pluck promising men and women out of their normal working lives and give them life-changing and career-making experiences. The fact that he looked only at talent, not at sex, allowed these commissions to stand out for their gender diversity. After all, in the old boys' clubs of the past, merit was not the major consideration, so it was only natural that someone who judged people instead by their talent and effectiveness would advance the roles of women and other hitherto outsiders.

"I always felt there were just as many bright females in the world as males," Purdy says in the video. "If we are not taking advantage of that, we are not getting all the talent we should have in business." It is pure Purdy—no sloganeering or sabre rattling. His message is that supporting women is a means to an end: better companies, a better economy, a better Canada. And that attitude toward mentoring and human development has been a force in cracking all kinds of ceilings. According to TD president Ed Clark, "he advocated women long before it was in vogue." At one time, women and Jews were not wanted in many law firms, but "Purdy only values what you are—and he is a tough marker, but a fair tough marker."

Crawford at times seems baffled with how he became known as a master mentor. It is not as though he held this up as his goal. He

just befriended people, and it led to giving them advice—whether it
was John Bragg or Wallace McCain or the guy at the service station.
He appreciated what Allan Beattie and the other lawyers at Osler
did for him. Later, he in turn was the dispenser of guidance at Osler,
where the partners would say to young lawyers, "why don't you talk
to Purdy about it?" Today, mentoring is a discipline, a buzzword, and
he accepts that people seek him out. "Young people come to me today
and are straightforward that they would like me to be their mentor."

He is not always accommodating. Recently, he got a letter from
a young Maritimer asking if Crawford could open doors for him in
Toronto. He complained that his university was not very good, and
he thought the Toronto business community discriminated against
Easterners. When asked if he could help, Purdy was direct: "Yes, get
the books out and get to work." He thought the young man's school
was just fine; moreover, "I haven't heard of someone in Atlantic
Canada discriminated against in Toronto. I was annoyed because he
was aggressive." "Aggressive" is Purdy's code word for obnoxious. He
tends to turn his back on people who are "aggressive." And sometimes
he has to tell people just to deal with it.

In a corporate world where women were dismissed as too light-
weight, too gentle, lacking the killer instinct, Purdy sees these as-
sumptions as not only spurious but trivial. He looks for brains, yes,
and commitment, but also fire in the belly—for "pistols" as he told
Annette Verschuren. She is Purdy's best-known project, but there are
many more. Purdy surrounds himself with smart women.

Lynn Loewen is watching the Catalyst event from one of the tables
at the Royal York, and she knows what the other women are talking
about. The Newfoundland-born Loewen, a chartered accountant and
Mount Allison grad, has known Purdy since the 1990s, when she was
pulled into the university's board and fundraising. Purdy has helped
guide her through a career that has spanned an East Coast airline,
telecommunications, and high-tech medical devices. On Purdy's

capacity to promote women, she says, "he did it before it was cool. Today you get evaluated on it as part of your performance."

Dale Ponder, managing partner at Osler, points out that she is the third woman to head the law firm since 1996, testimony to the momentous change since Bertha Wilson cracked the partner ceiling. The firm has grown to just under five hundred lawyers, compared with twenty-two when Purdy joined, and women made up a large percentage of the 2014 incoming partners, which suggests more change lies ahead. "Purdy had a lot to do with that," Ponder comments. "He has been a big part of our culture and our core values of excellence, leadership, and mentorship."

Why so many women among his mentees? "Sometimes I think it is because we have five daughters," Purdy says. "That probably resulted in my showing more interest in women lawyers at Osler and elsewhere." Even so, he worries that he wasn't proactive enough in advancing women, particularly in the family businesses he often advises. "Historically, the people who got the opportunity to go forward in a family business were the men; nobody thought of the women, [but] that is starting to change. We passed up a lot of opportunities not bringing women forward." Although his own daughters are successful in law (Suzanne and Heather), real estate (Mary), business consulting (Barbara), and corporate management (Sarah), "it's too bad we guys didn't treat our daughters equally, and that holds them back."

Purdy has a lot of male friends—old golfing buddies, baseball fans, investment cronies. He is a man's man—away from the office, he likes the company of men—but on the issue of talent, he is blind to the things that don't matter. It is not that he focuses just on women—his mentoring cuts across gender, race, class, religion. If he has a prejudice, it is in favour of people from his native Maritimes; there is no doubt that he sees himself in some of these young strivers from the Miramichi, Cape Breton, and the Annapolis Valley. But, according to his daughter Heather, there is an important distinction between mentoring and sponsorship. Purdy actually sponsors people, which is a more engaged advocacy than a simple note or two of support. The help can be multifaceted—a reference, a contact, a word of introduction, an exploration of options—or it can be nothing more than a recommendation of a book to read. There is no one-size-fits-all mentoring formula, but a customized approach that depends on what's needed.

In this work, he has brought a lot of women into his public service committees and task forces, and, he says, it was to some extent intentional. He sees himself as redressing the power imbalance in law firms and society. Women in the legal profession seem generally more interested in this public service work—they see the big picture. While male lawyers seem preoccupied with billable hours, women can see the longer-term rewards from public service and pro bono efforts—the kinds of below-the-radar activities that allow women to move ahead more quickly. They are, after all, what made Purdy Crawford, an outsider from a different era, a Bay Street powerhouse.

Take the case of "the most feared person on Bay Street," as described by *Toronto Life* magazine. That's Maureen Jensen, a financial markets regulator who is number ten on the magazine's 2013 list of Toronto's most influential people. Jensen, the executive director and chief administrative officer of the Ontario Securities Commission, is a tiger at going after people who violate insider trading rules and other standards that make the markets work. She is also one of the most powerful voices in favour of putting women on boards by pushing the OSC's "comply or explain" policy: if companies are not ready to support women, they should be required to explain why. Jensen, a geologist and daughter of a Falconbridge engineer, worked in the mining industry for twenty years before she became a regulator, and she is, quite naturally, a self-proclaimed follower of Purdy Crawford.

Jensen first met Purdy in 1999, when she was working at the Toronto Stock Exchange and became an adviser to a commission looking at the role of securities analysts in the wake of Wall Street scandals. Crawford led the commission. "I didn't know what to expect because he has huge, larger-than-life profile," Jensen says, "but he has a way about him that he listens to everyone regardless of viewpoint and engages them in way that they contribute more and start digging deeper." The two of them got along well. "He taught me about leadership in a team environment," she says, even though he came from what was ostensibly a command-and-control culture at Imasco. "He has this collegial manner around a core of iron," she noticed. "He is an incredible mentor and does it effortlessly. He's very generous with time when he works with women moving up through the ranks." He is also gentle in his guidance. When Jensen brings up an issue, he suggests the name of someone to whom she might want to speak. When he sees something about her in the press, he sends a congratulatory note or comment. Every once in a while, he passes on an article to read or a book suggestion. "If he says 'read this book,' there are five hundred people who go out and buy the book," she laughs.

Occasionally, Jensen goes to him. "I ask what to do next. At times I hit a crossroads." Jensen admits she is "a junkie for a steep learning curve." Purdy will sometimes advise her that the learning phase is the most enjoyable time in a job, when you are just sucking in the information. Enjoy it while you can. Jensen might say she is thinking about a certain job or opportunity, and he might support her inquiries—or suggest she explore something new in her own workplace. It is not a deeply personal relationship but advice from afar. When Purdy is frustrated, she sees not anger but "a controlled burn. It's all about that: how do you harness your fire?" Purdy's work ethic is legendary. Even so, Jensen in her job sees a lot of people who can work very hard. But in Purdy's case, it is the package of hard work and passion for the work: the fire.

Crawford is part of Catalyst's Women On Board mentoring program. That is how Nancy McKinstry found him. McKinstry, a Vancouver businesswoman, had an enviable business track record and was successful in getting on some big western Canadian boards, including the Canadian arm of the global bank HSBC, but she wanted to break into Ontario. Women On Board gave her a choice of potential mentors there, and having worked in the investment business she knew a bit about Crawford. He was her first choice.

"He was absolutely open and gave me as much time as I wanted," she says. It was not a long relationship, but a fulfilling one. McKinstry flew to Toronto five or six times to meet him. "He listened and asked very relevant questions that forced me to do some thinking. He never told me what to do. For me, that was the right way to handle it. He never lays his credentials out—he never says 'this is the way I would do it.' He never makes me feel I don't have the qualifications and capacity. I almost felt like I was in kindergarten because in Toronto no one knows you or your contributions. Being introduced by Purdy gave me a leg up," she says. She no longer goes to Purdy for help, but his name is golden in the right circles.

His mentorship is not limited to business; it also encompasses public service and politics. Nova Scotia MP Scott Brison has received financial and moral support from Crawford in both his political in-carnations—first as a Progressive Conservative and, after 2003, as a Liberal. Three years after crossing the floor of the House of Commons, Brison was considering a run at the Liberal leadership in the wake of Paul Martin's resignation, and he went to Crawford for advice. Purdy recommended against it, arguing that he had not been in the party long and it was a crowded field. Brison ran anyway but lost in the vote that made Stéphane Dion Liberal leader. Purdy supported Brison in any case. "All kinds of people will tell you what you want to hear," Brison says. "But Purdy was brutally honest then. It was an indication he could be counted on for unvarnished truth and critical thinking."

Also for puckish humour. It was on display in October 2005, when Brison invited two hundred people to the United Church in his home town of Cheverie, Nova Scotia, where he was marrying his partner, Maxime St-Pierre. The two men tried to keep the ceremony private, but word inevitably leaked out, and, on the day of the wedding, a media throng was assembling. Brison and St-Pierre used a decoy vehicle to lure away the press and sneaked into the church basement well ahead of the ceremony. It was all being made up on the fly. Here were, in Brison's words, "two men getting married in a weathered church in rural Nova Scotia."

As the guests came streaming in, one—Purdy Crawford—wandered downstairs in search of the washroom and came upon the couple. He dropped down on one knee and, with ceremonial flourish, kissed Brison's hand and congratulated him. It broke the tension, and Brison loved it.

In some cases, Purdy has applied his talent at guiding people's careers to the broad brush of an entire organization. That was his role at Imasco and, to some extent, at Canadian National. And it was in full bloom at Emera, the stock-market-listed holding company for Nova Scotia Power. Emera had gone through a tortured process of nationalization in 1973, then privatization in 1992. Purdy was a director from 1995 to 2004 and head of the board committee that oversaw people development.

As a senior manager, Chris Huskilson watched as Crawford helped the company evolve its management development program. "He guided us through the process where we went from a light-touch development-and-succession approach to a well-developed process. We now have one of the best leadership development processes in the country. That is what he is mostly known for—people development. He would touch so many people that way," he says. Purdy's role was not just about developing talent in isolation but as an essential piece in building capacity throughout the company to broaden its business model.

The legacy lives on as Emera embarks on its biggest challenge—as a partner in the massive Muskrat Falls hydro project in Labrador, which will take power through Newfoundland to the proposed Maritime Link connecting the island to Nova Scotia. Emera heralds the project as a game changer. "I would credit Purdy's work on capacity building—human and corporate," Huskilson says. "A large part of what he brought was a view of the private sector and how to evolve into a private company."

As Huskilson rose to be CEO of Emera, Purdy took on more of a one-to-one mentoring role. Huskilson, like McKinstry, discovered that Crawford lets people discover the right route on their own, but he does a lot of guiding. He does not say "do it this way," but "here is an opportunity." Huskilson sums up Crawford's key mentoring traits. First, he is astute in understanding what people need at a certain time of their development, and he is able to make a connection that is important. Second, he is extremely good at taking risks on people. He has a keen eye for people who have qualities that he thinks can evolve into much more. Third, it becomes a back-and-forth thing: when people respond to how he is trying to help them, he expands the conversation into a dialogue on leadership. Finally, he fills in the gaps: "I was an operator, engineer by training, and spent all my career hands-on in the field, and I needed to learn the corporate side," Huskilson says. "He had all that experience. And in everything, the one word you would describe him as is 'gentleman'."

Even in declining health, Purdy is always on the lookout for people, male or female, who can lead. But Purdy is not confined to the elite. While he can be the trusted mentor to a Michael McCain—the scion of a powerful family—there is an aspect of Purdy's work that clearly aims at balancing the power structure, at boosting unconventional, unlikely people and giving them the tools to become successful. He never forgets where he came from or the long, tortuous journey to where he is today.

Sean Foran, senior vice-president of an Edmonton company that sells rock crushers for the mining and oil industry, admits he is rough around the edges. He is an engineer in his early forties from the Miramichi region in New Brunswick, and his story sounds a bit like the tale of Purdy Crawford: a diamond in the rough, a Maritime boy with a rural accent and a compelling desire to get himself out there, meet people, and move up. He wanted to lose a few of the rough edges without losing his soul.

Foran is an enterprising sort. After high school in New Brunswick, he ran his own business in logging and construction before going back to school for engineering. When he graduated, he headed out west, following the dream of many Maritimers who see greater opportunities in the mining and energy pools there. When he approached his forties and began to think deeply about his career, someone suggested he should see this guy Purdy Crawford, who "kind of likes to help Maritimers succeed and do well." They met, and Purdy gave him a couple of contacts. But when Foran landed a much bigger job, he urgently needed help, and he sought out Purdy again.

"He's a good judge of character—he probably looked at me and thought I was pretty rough," Foran says. "He said, 'I think you need a mentor, more than just contacts'." But instead of taking Foran on, Crawford directed him to a seasoned female manager from the mining sector, who became his mentor. "He is all about exposing yourself and trying to make a reputation—so that there is something after this job. And to make you more of an all-rounder," says Foran, who has been so busy in the oil patch that he has had little time for career planning. But it will happen. Purdy got him started, and the extent to which he still keeps in touch baffles Foran. "I'm really a nobody, but he doesn't look at it that way."

Purdy never looks at it that way, in the people he finds and supports.

## Chapter Nine

# CODFATHER-IN-CHIEF

I t is a dull October day in the Toronto neighbourhood of Rosedale, home to rambling brick houses, tree-lined streets, and the people who run Canada. But in Margaret McCain's sunroom, it is all brightness and light colours, with comfortable sofas you can sink into for an afternoon. A Tom Forrestall painting of a stark white barn dominates one wall, perhaps reminding Margaret of her farm roots near Truro, Nova Scotia, and the tortuous odyssey that has taken her to Mount Allison University, to Florenceville, New Brunswick, and then, twenty years ago, to Toronto.

She has seen a lot: the family feud that turned her husband Wallace against his brother Harrison and other family members; the corporate struggles of her husband's and sons' Maple Leaf Foods; the public health crisis involving a Maple Leaf plant that caused twenty-two deaths; and the cancer that took away her husband, the love of her life. On top of all that has been her forceful advocacy of causes such as violence against women and early childhood education. Through it all, she says, "it gave me huge comfort knowing Purdy was there and to be trusting his integrity. Purdy had nothing to gain—it was built purely on friendship."

Of all his roles, the part Crawford has played in the affairs of the great Maritime entrepreneurs is probably his most fulfilling, rivalled

Young Purdy (five or six years old) with his father, Frank. 1935.

Purdy (right) with his roommate John Buchanan at Mount Allison. 1951.

"Babe" Corbett, as Bea was known then, with Purdy
at age sixteen or seventeen. 1949.

Bea and Purdy. 2012.

Purdy showing an Upper Canadian how to dig clams at Five Islands, N.S. 1977.

Left to right: James and Hal MacAloney, Purdy's brothers; Purdy;
Grace MacAloney, Purdy's mother; and Bea Crawford, Purdy's wife. 1990.

Purdy reading with his grandchildren, nine years ago (2003) and more recently. (2012).

The Imasco years. Left to right: Purdy, Brian Levitt, and Paul Paré. 1991.

Mount Allison Campaign dinner, 1987-88. Back row, left to right: Rod Bryden, Bea Crawford, Wallace McCain, Sue Winsor, Bob Winsor. Front row, left to right: Jim Lockyer, Margaret McCain, Don Wells, Purdy.

Chief Rising Tide. 2012.

With Governor General David Johnston, a dear friend, taken when Purdy was promoted to Companion of the Order of Canada. 2007.

Three Mount Allison chancellors. Left to right: Purdy, Margaret McCain, and John Bragg. 2005.

Purdy Crawford and John Bragg at Mount Allison donor appreciation dinner at Fox Harb'r, N.S. 2012.

Left to right: Dr. Robert Campbell, president and vice-chancellor of Mount Allison; Purdy, past chancellor; His Excellency the Right Honourable David Johnston, Governor General of Canada; Margaret McCain, past chancellor; and chancellor Peter Mansbridge. 2011.

only by his involvement in the asset-backed commercial paper crisis. He has been a kind of safety net, someone who can give unvarnished advice while staying resolutely loyal and preserving a friendship. John Bragg, the blueberries and cable TV czar, has been a steadfast friend; Purdy has been a director of David Ganong's chocolate company; he was a powerful voice in the evolution of Emera, the holding company of Nova Scotia Power. But perhaps his most significant contribution was to be a rock of support for Wallace and Margaret McCain. It is this story that displays the intermingling of the personal, the professional, the mentoring, and the geographical—for the McCains are still, at heart, Maritimers, and Purdy is above all a man with a deep devotion to the East Coast.

It is where you see the interlacing of Purdy's web of networks: corporate director, Mount Allison board member, fundraiser, and alumnus, legal advisor, loyal friend. In an earlier book, I used the term "codfathers" to refer not only to the mafia that control Down East business, but also to those who have gone away and made great careers but are drawn back to Maritime summer homes or to help out local businesses. There are many stars in this constellation, including former New Brunswick premier Frank McKenna; lawyer, director, and Margaret Thatcher's privatization guru, Sir Graham Day; Loblaw's builder Richard Currie; Nova Scotia investor and fisheries tycoon John Risley; Tim Hortons' co-founder Ron Joyce; and Kevin Lynch, former boss of the federal bureaucracy who is now vice-chair at BMO Financial Group.

But Purdy Crawford is the codfather-in-chief, who quietly, tenaciously, champions Maritimers no matter where they hang their hats—whether in small-town Atlantic Canada or big-town Toronto, Montreal, or Calgary.

TD Bank CEO Ed Clark talks about going to Frank McKenna's annual conference and golfing holiday, held each summer at Ron Joyce's Fox Harb'r resort, on the southern shore of the Northumberland Strait, and coming into a roomfull of East Coast titans—all billionaires except for the man at the head of the table, Purdy Crawford. The hierarchy is clear, and, as a reminder of who is really in charge here, Purdy dispatches the banker to get some Scotches for the group.

Crawford kept coming back—to the farmhouse where two of Bea's bachelor uncles lived for decades, a dark smoky place when Purdy and Bea bought it in the 1960s. Known as the Swinging Door, it became a gathering place for the clan. They added a sunroom along the back and a trove of family photos and antiques. The Crawfords also have a country place at Caledon, outside Toronto—a modernist building called the Whitehouse—and a high-rise condo along the Gulf of Mexico in Naples, Florida. But summer means a return to Five Islands. In time, the family would outgrow the farmhouse, and Purdy's daughters and Bea would direct the building of a much bigger place a short drive east and down by the water. It was near completion as this book was going to press.

All these associations come together in the story of the McCains, particularly brothers Wallace and Harrison, the ambitious offspring of a Saint John River Valley potato farmer and seed-potato exporter. The two worked a while for New Brunswick industrialist K. C. Irving but developed a passion for building their own business—and their brother Bob suggested a new concept, frozen french fries, would be the next big thing. The factory started up in the late 1950s in the McCains' hometown of Florenceville, New Brunswick, and it hitched onto the shooting star of the global fast food industry, serving busy families and two-income couples that needed to prepare meals in a hurry. McCain Foods in time would supply a third of the world's french fries and, by the late 1980s, was a multinational with operations in the United States, Europe, Australia, and Asia and venturing into food products from orange juice to frozen desserts.

"Harrison was the upfront person and Wallace the operator, although he could deal with people, too," Purdy once recalled in an interview for the *Globe and Mail*. "They were quite a team—they built an organization around the world from a base in Florenceville. They would take off Sunday night or Monday morning from the airstrip and come back Thursday or Friday if they were lucky."

But a difference of opinion began to simmer between the two brothers; by the early 1990s, it was a full-fledged dispute and then all-out war. As is common in such family quarrels, it was about succession. Wallace figured his younger son Michael, a bright young business school graduate, was best equipped to lead the company in the future. Harrison did not, and the partnership was falling apart.

In need of the most trusted and confidential kind of advice, Wallace turned to Purdy Crawford, then still CEO of Imasco and a key partner with Wallace and Margaret in the nurturing of Mount Allison University. And Purdy had someone in mind who could help Wallace: his old Osler colleague, a savvy senior lawyer named Jack Petch.

One day in 1990, Petch was sitting in his Osler office, wrapped up in a big case, when he was told that Wallace McCain was calling from Australia. "Who the hell is Wallace McCain?" Petch thought. Then he recalled a conversation about McCain he'd had earlier with Purdy and decided he should speak to this guy. They agreed to meet, and Petch was immediately attracted to this larger-than-life figure with a knack for creative profanity. Wallace's first line was: "What do you know about family fights, Jack?"

Petch actually knew a bit. He had done a lot of work with a business family embroiled in a dynastic dispute, and he knew that a lawyer in this context needed to develop trust and respect. He decided to take the job on—it would be the start of a long and valuable relationship for both sides. He would be a pillar for Wallace during the estrangement, but more than that, he would become a director, trusted advisor, and family foundation head for the future. When he retired from Osler, he would take an office in the McCains' midtown Toronto office building, a few floors down from Michael McCain.

First, though, he was immediately thrust into what the McCains call "the war." To outsiders, it was sad, tragic even, but disturbingly fascinating, like a multicar pileup on an urban expressway. Journalists couldn't take their eyes off it, as the McCain brothers and cousins battled it out. For Purdy, it was wrenching, and he didn't want to pick sides, but Wallace was his friend, and from that moment on he figured prominently in Wallace's life and that of Margaret McCain, whom he knew at Mount A as a student and now as a fellow Mount A board member and fundraiser. Wallace also turned aspects of Michael's career development over to Purdy. Michael became one of the veteran lawyer's projects and perhaps his most challenging because of Michael's package of a good mind, a passion for business, and a polarizing personality.

By the mid-1990s, the McCains' dispute had become an en-trenched struggle between Wallace's side of the family and Harrison and the offspring of the other brothers. Harrison and his camp took action to expel Wallace, Michael, and Scott McCain from McCain Foods. Jack Petch helped the Wallace side enlist a crack litigator, Alan Lenczner, and a highly publicized legal battle was fought out in Fredericton. The outcome left Wallace without a company; although he still held his one-third interest in McCain Foods, he was no longer part of its management or direction.

What to do next? The McCains were deeply rooted in the Maritimes. Margaret was part of the Mount A fabric and had been appointed the first female lieutenant-governor of New Brunswick, but business was Wallace's and his sons' very essence. They thought about going to the United States or even Australia, which Wallace had got to know well in establishing McCain Foods there. In the end they decided to team up with the Ontario Teachers' Pension Plan in 1995 to buy Maple Leaf Foods, an old and somewhat decrepit meat packer, food processor, and marketer. Maple Leaf's status as a public company made Wallace more dependent than ever on Purdy Crawford, who knew how to navigate around the difficult shoals of Bay Street. Maple Leaf was an untidy collection of businesses—not just a meat packing and marketing organization, but also a successful bread company and a player in animal feed—and it needed help from someone who knew how to run a multi-unit business. Purdy joined the McCains in two capacities: as a director of McCain Capital, the family holding company, and on the board of Maple Leaf Foods. Wallace was installed as chairman and Michael as president and CEO.

For Margaret McCain, emotionally drained from the family war and now suddenly planning a move to Toronto, it was comforting to know Purdy was there as the family took over Maple Leaf and began to deal with a whole new set of problems. She admits she is a bit of an ostrich when things get rough, and she could keep her head buried with Purdy around. "It gave me a huge sense of comfort," Margaret says.

From that relationship grew an even closer friendship between the two families. Margaret and Wallace and Purdy and Bea travelled together, often with John Bragg and Frank McKenna and their spouses, or with David and Donald Sobey and their wives. There were cruises to the Caribbean and the Mediterranean, where Purdy would impress with his love of dancing and his devotion to information. While the others sunned themselves on deck, Purdy often could be found squirrelled away with a book or a pile of newspapers picked up at the last port of call.

But Purdy's essential role lay in advising Wallace and mentoring Michael, now the CEO of his own company and teamed up with his tall and amiable older brother Scott. For Scott, it was a chance to watch a master at work. He was not, like Michael, a direct student of Purdy's, but he enjoyed watching the lawyer's moderating influence on his father and brother in what he calls the "postwar era." Purdy always tries to look for the positive; he never wants to fight. "He would always encourage ways not to burn bridges with McCain Foods," Scott recalls.

"My father was still bruised, but Purdy always said 'take the high road and try to build bridges,' and that's what happened." Over the years, the tension between the family sides would remain raw, but in time Wallace and Harrison took steps to repair their relationship. By the time Harrison died in March 2004, they had become close again. His death was a double tragedy— it was not just the loss of a huge, vital personality, but it also ended the new closeness of the McCain boys.

Through it all, Scott says, "Purdy was always the voice of reason and compromise. Michael and Dad would get edgy, but Purdy would say 'you might need these guys some day'." What's more, Crawford would often play a conciliatory role between father and son, who, as two strong personalities, loved each other but would sometimes clash. Michael equates Crawford to that old TV commercial by the now long-departed stock brokerage firm: "When E. F. Hutton speaks, people listen." In the boardroom, when Purdy spoke, conversation, however raucous, would dull down. "He has the rare gift of having a lot of influence but being very precise—he never overspoke, and when he had an opinion, it was good. Even when [he was] giving you hell, you felt good about it."

Maple Leaf Foods was a roller coaster, and Michael as CEO had to deal with a barrage of challenges: changing markets, a fluctuating Canadian dollar, and activist shareholders who took big positions and advocated changes, including breaking up the business. He kept turning to Crawford for advice. "For the first five years when I was CEO, we had a meal once a month," Michael says. They would talk about the issues, and Purdy would coach him. "He would definitely give you hell, any mentor does." By now, Michael was focusing on Maple Leaf and turning his back on McCain Foods, where Wallace and his family still held a one-third interest. Michael remembers that "Purdy would always say, 'Look, Michael, for you to be as successful as I feel you deserve to be, you have to create a higher level of independence. You are going to have to lean into some risk in your life.' At the end of the day, we accomplished both." In time, Michael made a full break from the old family firm and focused all his capital and attention on Maple Leaf, and Purdy supported him. "His perspective is 'this is where you have made your life—all in or all out'," Michael says.

Crawford also had a realistic view of the family dynamics, recognizing that Michael was a central issue in the tension at McCain Foods and that he should stay away from it entirely. Michael was a lightning rod blessed—and burdened—with a personality that naturally takes charge. Scott McCain says, "Purdy was one of the early ones to counsel Michael to take risks and build his own legacy. He said it was hard to build that legacy in McCain Foods, but you can do it in Maple Leaf." Scott, for his part, was moving in the other direction, back to the old family business.

Inside Maple Leaf, Purdy applied the lesson he had learned at Osler and Imasco: you are only as strong as the people in your organization. From the moment Michael took over as CEO in 1998, Crawford prodded him to make people development the single biggest focus of his leadership role. It is a hard thing to track, but the events of summer 2008 are, in many ways, a legacy of Purdy's impact on the organization.

In August 2008, public health officials reported an outbreak of listeria, a food-borne bacteria that can result in severe illness and death. By late that month, the contamination was traced to a Maple Leaf Foods factory in Toronto, which prompted a massive national recall of the company's packaged meats. Over the next few months, Michael McCain became the man in the hot seat. He performed well. His combination of taking total responsibility, displaying visible concern for the victims, and maintaining communications with stakeholders and the public made him a model for crisis management that would be studied at business schools.

In all, twenty-two people died and many more got sick from the listeria outbreak, one of the most dire public health crises in

Canadian history. The illness was particularly dangerous to the very elderly, who had the most vulnerable immune systems, and pregnant women. The outbreak triggered a spate of class action law suits, and the media focused hard on the gaps in Canada's food inspection system. Customers turned to other meat sources, delivering a blow to the company's bottom line, which was already feeling the effects of the financial meltdown that was battering the global economy. Maple Leaf could never erase its responsibility for the tragic result of the listeria outbreak, but it came through the crisis with its reputation still intact, if somewhat frayed.

As a director of Maple Leaf, Purdy was supportive, but the crisis was an operational issue and a communications challenge and did not call for his direct involvement. But it is hard to believe that Michael McCain's display of emotional depth, leadership, and communication skills would have been possible without the decade of coaching by Purdy Crawford.

Wallace, too, stayed in the background—it was now Michael's show. In a 2009 interview, I asked Wallace to summarize his tumultuous career. "The biggest thing that happened to me in the past twenty-five years—and in my life—was being unceremoniously dumped from McCain Foods." And the second biggest, he said, was the listeria crisis of 2008. "My son Michael had a plan to make this company competitive even with a high Canadian dollar. We had made twenty-five to thirty acquisitions, and the plan was to bring it down to four or five businesses. It meant closing small factories, merging companies together, installing a new computer system. We were eight months into the plan when all those other things blew up. In addition to the dollar, wheat went up, corn went up, and oil went up. All this had happened and then the listeria crisis struck. The combination hit Maple Leaf Foods right between the eyes."

But he admitted that it was not his company any more. "Michael runs this company, and he is an independent guy. If I want to give

him advice, he will say thank you and he might take it or he might
not. That's exactly what I want him to do. It's his responsibility, his
ballgame, his deal." Wallace remained chair of the board, but he
was not long for this role. He was stricken by pancreatic cancer, and
although he searched for a way to arrest or slow down the disease,
he died in May 2011 at age eighty-one after a fourteen-month battle
with the illness.

It was a period of intense pressure for Michael McCain. He not
only suffered a profound personal loss; he had also been dealing with
a new age in governance. Maple Leaf was never a big money maker,
and the economic and operational challenges weighed heavily on its
stock price. The McCains' long-time partner, the Ontario Teachers'
Pension Plan, let it be known that it wanted to divest all or part of its
36 percent stake. Meanwhile, activist investors clamoured for changes,
and that outcry often focused on demands to blow up the board.

The most prominent agitator was Greg Boland, head of the
Toronto-based hedge fund West Face Capital, who had scored victor-
ies in boosting the values of underperforming companies. In August
2010, he spent $113 million to purchase a 10 percent stake in Maple
Leaf—part of the former Ontario Teachers' holding—and immediately
met with Michael to demand some explanation of when his long-term
strategy to overhaul the company would deliver the long-promised
turnaround. On December 3, 2010, West Face called for a meeting of
shareholders to vote for a smaller board of new directors that would
not be dominated by McCain family friends and associates. "The
deficiencies of Maple Leaf in critical areas such as board independence
and corporate governance are well known," West Face said.

In questioning the board's independence, Boland took dead aim
at Purdy Crawford, questioning whether he was truly independent
of the ownership family. He was not a family member or an executive
with Maple Leaf, but his friendship with Wallace went back to their
Mount Allison days, and his youngest daughter Sarah worked for

Maple Leaf Foods. Boland's campaign was an affront to Crawford, the dean of corporate directors and the face of principled corporate governance in Canada. It became a case study of the delicate issue of independence on boards. Yet, even as he was under attack, Purdy continued to provide stability, and he encouraged Michael to come to terms with West Face. In February 2011, Boland and Michael made peace, although Michael had little choice—a survey of investors revealed that the hedge fund had enough support to win its proxy contest. Maple Leaf announced that Boland had agreed to join its board, and the company would accelerate its promised reorganization. The battle was not personal—it was hard-nosed business. Scott equates Boland to famous hockey agitator Ken Linseman (a.k.a. The Rat), who played for the Philadelphia Flyers, Edmonton Oilers, and Boston Bruins in the 1980s: "He stirs the pot and creates anxiety." Scott continues, though, that "some would be insulted, but Purdy moves on. It's beyond role modelling—it is leadership by way of example."

The debate over Crawford's role became a case study in how the new rules of governance, with their emphasis on independence, should be applied in the bare-knuckles arena of the market, with its new breed of activists. Michael McCain aggressively questions this focus on a narrow definition of independence. What matters, he says, is the quality of the people, not the box-ticking of credentials. He insists that good friends of the CEO can be counted on to give more prudent advice. In fact, Michael maintains, friends can be trusted to be more frank and honest than outsiders who have less on the line.

As a test of board independence, the West Face campaign against Purdy Crawford was "an extraordinary travesty of that process," Michael insists. "Purdy and his integrity and reputation were too important to him, my father, and me to ever allow the fact there was some history to get in the way of doing things right." West Face's questioning of Purdy Crawford's role was more than an unfortunate collateral tactic; it was simply wrong, Michael says. "The history of

Purdy's tenure was that he was always the advocate, the custodian, the godfather of governance in this organization."

Purdy's take on it is, as usual, measured. He notes that Greg Boland apologized to him later. "It didn't really trouble me that much. What bothered me was I wanted to go public and deal with my own case, and tell the world what was going on." Instead, Maple Leaf Foods and its public relations people said that, as a director, he should not comment. He echoes the McCains' view that he has given some of his best advice to people who didn't want to hear it, but they were willing to take it because he is a friend. That was his role with Maple Leaf. As for the West Face incident, "it was part of the game, but I would have liked to have run the show, instead of Michael. I'm not used to being in the back seat." In 2011, Purdy retired from the board of Maple Leaf. "At the end of it, I became eighty, and I said it is time to pack it in, with or without the problem." Boland was not a bad guy, but he was just playing the game. Purdy could live with that, even if he was hurt.

He remained deeply involved in some boards, particularly in the Maritimes, where he has always played a role. One of those board roles arose, as with the McCains, from a valued personal relationship. Years earlier, as he and Margaret McCain were settling into the board and fundraising roles at Mount Allison, Purdy got to know another Mount A alumnus, a rising entrepreneur named John Bragg.

Bragg's story is an improbable one. As a young Mount Allison student and aspiring teacher—he attended university eight years after Purdy—he spent the summers gathering wild blueberries from the woodlots owned by his forestry industry family. Soon, he was pulling in thousands of dollars from blueberries and discarding his teaching dreams. He built the largest wild blueberry producer in the world, as well as a frozen food business that got a springboard from supplying onion rings to the McCain Foods empire. Then, in the early 1970s, he took a flyer on some cable TV licences in Nova Scotia and eventually grew those into a cable, Internet, and broadband complex called Eastlink, which is expanding nationwide and bidding to become the next big pillar of Canadian communication, along with BCE, Rogers, Telus, and Quebecor. Very quietly he amassed a collection of businesses with $1 billion in annual sales out of little Oxford, Nova Scotia.

As the crow flies, it is not far from the old Bragg family home in Collingwood Corner, near Oxford, southwest to Purdy Crawford's hometown of Five Islands, but there is no direct highway link, so people in Five Islands don't necessarily know people in Collingwood Corner. Bragg and Crawford, though, were brought together because of their university roles. University boards in places such as the Maritimes are not just about governance; they are important networking tools. Schools such as Mount A, St. Francis Xavier, the University of New Brunswick, Dalhousie, and Acadia serve that role well—there is the sense of being thrown together in an important cause.

As they got to know each other on the Mount A board, Purdy urged the younger man to become more active at the university as a fundraiser and leader, but Bragg couldn't see what value he could possibly bring. The two men and their wives went to dinner, and Purdy wasn't taking no for an answer. He cajoled Bragg into chairing the university's executive committee and, in time, Bragg would become chancellor, a redoubtable fundraiser, and a major player in ensuring the university's financial resilience and academic track record. In turn, Crawford joined the Oxford Frozen Foods advisory board in the early 1990s. Oxford is a private company, so Purdy's independence is never an issue here.

Crawford and Bragg became the closest of friends. They would travel together, whether a whirlwind visit to Bragg's far-flung blueberry empire, spending time with a valued customer in Japan, or on board Don Sobey's plane to attend Warren Buffett's annual clambake in Omaha. But the important link is the quiet counsel.

John Bragg says Purdy always supports his intellectual growth through reading: "He is always stretching to make you think outside the box."

In addition, although Purdy cut his teeth advising publicly traded companies on their governance and writing the rules of securities trading, he readily grasps what a private company is about. He understands the challenges of undertaking acquisitions by relying on bank lending and becoming heavily debt leveraged, as a fast-growth private company needs to do. "He was onside in not being afraid of leverage," Bragg says, "and in keeping equity in my own hands. It is very helpful to have a senior person like that understand what I was trying to do and be supportive."

One of Crawford's core tenets is the need for leaders to get outside their accustomed niches. He was always pushing Bragg to do more than he was comfortable with, convinced he would be a better leader internally if he were active outside. Soon, at Purdy's urging, Bragg was on a number of boards. Crawford would say "take it, take it—you will build a better management team if you are out of the company more." Bragg was an outstanding pupil. He wanted to be a good professional manager in a private company. In time, the pupil became knowledgeable, and it became more of a two-way street. That's a constant theme in Purdy's mentorship: the pupil becomes the teacher. And the Bragg assets have grown exponentially. Without Purdy, Bragg would have been successful—no doubt about it. With Purdy, he has become a fully formed business leader who commands respect far beyond the walls of his companies.

It is a similar story around the Maritimes. Purdy was briefly on the board of John Risley's Clearwater Foods; he helped David Ganong in his chocolate business in St. Stephen, New Brunswick; and even in his eighties was a director of LED Roadway, a private company in Halifax trying to burst into international markets for lighting systems for airport runways, roads, and offices of all kinds. He just liked the experience.

His concern for the region extends beyond the personal. Purdy has always seen the need for fresh approaches to Atlantic Canada's long-standing economic lethargy. "A lot of people in the region have too much of a look-after-us attitude," he told me in an interview in 2000. "The people are great and hard working, but well meaning governments have created a sense of dependence." He concedes it is a difficult balancing act when there are people who need help. "But the reality is that so many parts of Atlantic Canada turn on getting enough time in to get your unemployment insurance. And that's the best thing they have going for them. And the other thing that's the best thing is going to Ottawa to get money for this and that."

He was supportive when Halifax lawyers George Cooper and Bill Mingo teamed up with policy analyst Brian Lee Crowley to form the Atlantic Institute for Market Studies (AIMS), which provides an alternative voice to the heavy, government-directed, top-down policies that had dominated economic development. When the trio were pondering Purdy's appointment to their board, Crowley recalls that he asked idly what his politics were. Cooper, a former Tory MP, said Purdy was a Liberal; Mingo, a staunch Liberal, insisted he was a Conservative. "He always played those cards close to his vest," Crowley says. "I don't think party politics would be Purdy's thing." (Purdy later served on the advisory board of Crowley's latest think tank, the nationally focused Macdonald-Laurier Institute in Ottawa, while he was still chairman emeritus of AIMS.)

Also, Purdy manages to maintain credibility in Atlantic Canada, which can be unforgiving to people—actors or musicians—who move away and attain celebrity elsewhere, then come back and act "big feeling." "The Atlantic culture doesn't like people who put on airs," Crowley says. But Purdy wears his mover-and-shaker status lightly, and his work with people and companies in the region allows him to escape the commonly heard jibe of being a big shot "from away." One friend notes that the Toronto crowd with summer homes in Atlantic

Canada generally clusters in up-market enclaves south of Halifax such as Chester and Mahone Bay. Purdy, however, still headed home to Five Islands, where he reunites with local people and relatives every summer.

He jousts with John Bragg about the proper role of government, but it is not a profound disagreement—just a matter of shading and, as friends, they love to spar a bit. Bragg is a terrier on the issue of rural development and the need to stimulate economic growth outside the urban centres. It is vital for a balanced Canadian economy to develop an industrial base in the countryside, he argues. Purdy supports Bragg's work but is less certain about government's role. As he worked with AIMS, he began to think about rural Nova Scotia. He agreed with a number of Maritimers that the answer lay in private sector development, and often that means less, not more, government.

He and Bragg were both admirers of Frank McKenna, whose decade as New Brunswick premier was a case study in activist government aimed at developing a private sector that can flourish after the public money runs out. McKenna left the premier's job in 1997 and decided to divide his law practice between Moncton—where he was engaged with the firm Stewart McKelvey—and Toronto. There were a lot of options among law firms in Toronto but he ended up at Osler. "Purdy was very persuasive," McKenna says. After all, Purdy was then back at Osler, and the law firm was doing work for the Irvings, the McCains, and others in Atlantic Canada.

Later, McKenna left private life to become a successful Canadian ambassador to Washington. When he came back to Toronto again, there were entreaties for him to become the federal Liberal leader. He would very likely have ended up as prime minister, but he and his wife were not sure they wanted such an intense public life. And Frank was being wooed by Ed Clark to be TD Bank Group's deputy chair and an important bridge builder for the bank. Clark enlisted a number of high-placed friends to do his bidding. Purdy was one of them, and the lawyer would talk to McKenna about Ed Clark, "who was one of his people," McKenna notes. As a TD executive, McKenna became a ubiquitous networker to business and government.

Sometimes, the influences are subtle, the product of relationships bred in friendship and counsel. That is Crawford's link to the Sobeys—namely, brothers Donald and David, men about his age who grew up in Stellarton, Nova Scotia, less than two hours away by car from Five Islands. Established by their father Frank Sobey, the family supermarket chain grew under the brothers and took a dramatic upsurge in 1998 with the purchase of the Oshawa Group, which supplied stores under the IGA brand in much of Canada. Then, in 2013, the Sobeys staged another company-making coup: the purchase of the Canadian Safeway grocery empire, which gave them a strong western Canadian presence.

I met with David and Donald Sobey in December 2013 in a hotel in Port Credit, Ontario, where the board of the family holding company, Empire, was meeting. David and Donald are close, but they have complementary interests and skills. David is the supreme retailer, a real grocery store merchant, while Donald is seen as the consummate investor. Both were eloquent about what Crawford meant to them. David talked warmly about first meeting Purdy in the 1980s when they were both directors of Domtex, a big Canadian textile company challenged by changing times and free trade. "I came into the room, and there was Purdy. I got the feeling I'd known this guy for a long time even though this was the first meeting. He had that kind of disarming smile that made you relax." Brother Donald chimed in: "He is like a cuddly bear."

Purdy and David later served together on the board of Sydney Steel, the embattled Cape Breton manufacturer controlled by the province. David was part of a push for more private sector directors, and Crawford joined the board. In all these tasks, David Sobey noted that Purdy somehow lifted the conversation, taking it above the details to the big picture. "When you meet him, he disarms you. I wish I had met him earlier in life. I could have used that mentoring."

And he made a lot of money for the Sobeys by drawing their company into a 40 percent ownership interest in Genstar Development, for which they are forever beholden to him. As Imasco was being broken up, there were takers for the big pieces—Canada Trust, Shoppers—but not for the little-known property development arm. The Sobeys had partnered with Genstar in some projects, but this time Purdy came after them to buy a chunk of the company. And Purdy was personally borrowing money to come in as an investor, as well as attracting some Toronto interests led by developer Rudy Bratty.

Purdy explained that Genstar's great attributes were its large residential land holdings and management's stellar reputation with planning boards, which meant it could get property rezoned. Donald knew Crawford's track record, and he urged the family holding company's CEO, David's son Paul, to "take as much as you can. I knew if Purdy was in it, it would be good." At the time, the Sobeys were investing in shopping-centre real estate, and this new initiative would be a diversification into residential land. "Boy, did it ever work out!" Donald says. Genstar Development was consistently profitable under the guidance of CEO Frank Thomas, and it made a lot of money for the Sobeys—and for Purdy.

Genstar did well in Canada and in the hot US markets. But when prices rocketed in the bubble atmosphere of the 2000–07 period, Thomas saw the danger and, in 2007, sold off his positions in the United States. It was a superb bet of the kind the owners had come to expect from Thomas. He explains his timing: in the years leading up to the crash, "what I saw was a fairy tale. Whenever you thought you'd make a buck, you'd make $2.50. I figured this couldn't go on." After the market turned bad and foreclosures soared in the United States, Genstar found itself free and clear of the carnage. As well, its Canadian property business was still generating good cash, which Thomas used to go back into the United States to buy land at bargain-basement prices. By 2013, as values were coming back, Genstar was already well established again in US markets.

Investors were happy. The strategy helped Sobeys, under the umbrella of the Empire holding company, to diversify the real estate part of its business, which already included commercial property. In 2006, the commercial property assets were spun off in a real estate investment trust known as Crombie. As it prepared to absorb Canada Safeway, Empire was able to raise valuable cash by selling off the Safeway stores' real estate to Crombie. And the grocery business was also poised to divest its interests in Genstar Development, but with a certain regret—the residential developer had been a fantastic investment and one of the seeds of its strong real estate presence. "If Safeway hadn't come along, I think we wouldn't have sold [Genstar]. It's not like that business will disappear, but we had to do other things," David explains.

The Genstar Development story was a little-appreciated part of Sobeys' success, but in a sense it stemmed from Purdy Crawford's ability to spot leaders such as Frank Thomas. "It was about people, and Purdy got the people," Donald says admiringly.

## Chapter Ten

# GIVING AND GETTING

xit the TransCanada Highway at Sackville, New Brunswick, and drive south into the town. Just before the road takes a long, sweeping turn to the left, cutting into the campus of Mount Allison University, there looms, straight ahead, a new building in the rose-coloured sandstone brick that dominates the 175-year-old institution. It is the Purdy Crawford Centre for the Arts—the most tangible evidence of the man who has protected, nurtured, and built this school. This is the university that made Purdy, and it is the school he has fashioned—with big help from other donors, university presidents, board members, academics, staff employees, and, of course, generations of students. He has made it fiscally strong and academically gifted, allowing it to hit far above its weight, with a knack for turning out Rhodes Scholars and scoring as the best undergraduate university in Canada for seventeen of the past twenty-three years, as measured by *Maclean's* magazine.

The $30 million Centre, designed by the Toronto firm Zeidler Partnership Architects, will provide places for teaching, performance, and creative pursuits. It will be one of Mount Allison's signature buildings, an indelible image of the university for visitors. As a cultural and artistic showpiece, it is important for a small university that emphasizes the liberal arts and fine arts as a necessary grounding for leaders. Time after time, Purdy Crawford has entered a corporate CEO's office and laid out the plausible argument that, to succeed in the world—indeed, to lead—young people must have the battery of leadership skills, artistic exposure, and critical thinking that only a superb liberal arts program can deliver. And the postscript is that the Centre is being built without an iota of government funding.

Purdy's touches are everywhere: in a remarkable teaching centre for faculty members, for example, and in an award for staff service that, amid the entirely laudable teaching honours, recognizes the role of a secretary, a lab worker, or a staff photographer. It is the most striking example of the Purdy principles of philanthropy, fundraising, and public activism, with its focus on education and universities, which has extended to his transformative role at other universities. Without him, there would be no Purdy Crawford Chair in Business Law at Dalhousie or a Purdy Crawford Chair in Aboriginal Business Studies at Cape Breton University in Sydney.

He has been a modernizer in the university sector, in the same way he helped change the legal profession, the corporate boardroom, and capital market regulation. Mount Allison, as a small university with a long history of low-key, highly personalized leadership, might have been swamped by the tsunami of change in the 1970s and 1980s, as it confronted unionization, heftier government involvement, funding pressures, and competition for student bodies. Those challenges arose just as Purdy was re-entering the university's life as a successful alumnus. He led the wave to higher professionalization in the board and administration. As at Osler, he influenced the leadership selection in his search for people with merit who could appreciate both the works of the intellectual greats and the work being done on the bottom line. He knew unions would not go away, that they would have to be accommodated without giving away the keys to the place. His stewardship became a blueprint for the survival of the small university, a challenge that has been tackled at other quality schools such as St. Francis Xavier, Acadia, and Bishop's.

As a member of the board of regents, he helped guide Mount Allison through some of its financially challenged years, always trying to keep above the labour strife that pitted staff and faculty members against the administration. He supported the selection of Ian Newbould as president in the 1990s, a period when the university was reeling from deficit financing and needed a tough administrator to ensure its status—indeed, its survival. And he has left his imprint through the people he has urged to join the board and become active. He did not do it all alone, but a measure of his impact, in 2013, is a $130 million endowment and the total absence of university debt.

Mount Allison might be small, with fewer than three thousand students, but its history is that of a distinguished pioneer. Its roots reach back to 1839, when Sackville merchant Charles Frederick Allison proposed the creation of a school of elementary and higher learning. Hence, the Mount Allison Academy, a school for boys, was launched in 1843, followed by the Ladies College in 1854. The first degree-earning class in 1863 had just two graduates. The college was first associated with the Methodist Church and, after church union in the 1920s, the United Church. When young Purdy Crawford arrived, it was losing its ecclesiastical influences and was emerging as a non-denominational liberal arts school. It has always been in the forefront of social change, as the first university in the British Empire to award a bachelor's degree to a woman (Grace Annie Lockhart, Bachelor of Science, 1875), and the first university in Canada to grant a Bachelor of Arts to a woman (Harriet Starr Stewart, 1882).

But in the early 1970s, as an independent university, Mount Allison had to get serious about fundraising. It hired a young lawyer and development officer, a Canadian with US experience named Harvey Gilmour. Gilmour headed off to Toronto to look up one of the university's rising alumni, a young lawyer named Purdy Crawford. Crawford's firm, Osler, Hoskin & Harcourt, was the corporate law firm in Canada for Coca-Cola, and Mount A had the soft drink giant in its sights as a donor. After meeting Crawford, however, the association soon went far beyond Coke. "He became involved in my life and the university," Gilmour recalls. Encouraged by the young development officer, Purdy ultimately would join the Mount Allison board. At that point, he just wanted to help—there was no sense that he was going to become the life force of the place.

Crawford started making fundraising calls on behalf of Mount A, but found "it was hell early on asking people. Eventually you become used to it, particularly if you were running a campaign and knew what you had to do. I had a reputation of being a great fundraiser—I'm not sure there aren't better ones." There are great donors and great fundraisers, Purdy discovered, and they are not necessarily the same people. He learned to be good at both. The two activities feed each other: the fundraiser gets the donor to give to a cause; in return, the fundraiser feels obligated to support the donor's own cause. It becomes an ever-widening circle of giving and receiving. Crawford has recruited people to the Mount A board who did not score highly as fundraisers. But he found they often had unexpected talents—perhaps they were good with students and in building the collective purpose that good universities must nurture. He found ways to draw on talent, in whatever package it came.

At Mount Allison, Purdy worked hard to make would-be donors feel they were part of the campaign, part of a great project. Some people wanted their names on buildings or rooms, others couldn't care less. Indeed, Purdy did not really lobby to have the Mount A arts centre named after him—he would have named it after his friend and co-conspirator John Bragg. "I'm more interested in scholarships, professors, and the quality of faculty," he says. But he knows that his name can be a magnet for other donations.

And he was more than a fundraiser. During the 1970s and 1980s, heightened union activism put strains on the university and its atmosphere of quiet collegiality. Mount Allison was one of the first Canadian campuses where newly unionized faculty pushed aggressively for higher compensation. It was not enough reward, faculty members felt, to live in bucolic small-town Sackville; they demanded the same compensation as faculty received in bigger centres. But these demands came at a time when the university was suffering financial setbacks from restrained government funding and had begun to tap its endowment funds—basically meeting present needs by stealing from tomorrow.

Crawford never voiced his opinion for or against campus unions, but, according to someone close to the scene, he supported tighter control of finances, which he saw as necessary for the university's future. Margaret McCain, a former chancellor, remembers keenly when the selection committee met to discuss the choice of a new president in the winter of 1990–91. As the university board grappled with the need to draw the line on spending, the name of Ian Newbould came forward. Here was an experienced administrator, late of Lethbridge University in Alberta, with a reputation as a hard-liner on costs. But first, Newbould would have to be appointed, and that was no sure thing. As a member of the highly polarized selection committee, which included faculty, students, and alumni, Crawford listened to all sides but chose not to tip his hand, which made some who supported the Newbould appointment feel nervous. Margaret McCain says she remembers going to the washroom and putting her head up against the wall. "I wondered, Purdy, how are you going to vote? I should have known." It was typical of Purdy, the great listener, but in the end he voted with the majority in hiring Newbould.

In 1994, Crawford became chancellor of Mount Allison. Although it was more a face-of-the-university role, "he was always powerful behind the scenes," Ian Newbould recalls. "He was wonderful in fundraising; he was able to raise funds and we raised funds in his name." And he quietly backed Newbould's attempt to rein in the deficit. After three years, Newbould had eliminated the accumulated deficit, but at a cost: "I was cast as the bad guy," Newbould allows.

Indeed, Newbould's presidency would be a decade of upheaval with a series of bitter strikes, but the university and its unions weathered the storm. All through it, Purdy tried to play a moderating role. "Purdy always understood the need for aligning yourself with the culture," Newbould says. "To be a leader, your vision and their vision had to come together. He was often worried that my vision and the faculty's vision were going in different directions. The other board members didn't worry but Purdy did. If you're going to be a leader, [he felt], you will have to persuade them to follow." Newbould believes total amity would have been impossible during his time as president, given the financial crisis, the intensity of feeling, and the labour unrest. And Crawford worried about the atmosphere left by the strikes. He felt Newbould was a good president, but, he adds, he could be "a bull in his own china shop." In the final analysis, Purdy says, Newbould was "a good thing for Mount A." Labour relations would never be easy, but the university came out of the era in good shape.

Frank McKenna, as premier of New Brunswick during that tumultuous time, recalls that Mount Allison faced a barrage of financial and labour pressures, but it did not ask for a lot of help from the province—only that it be allowed to charge what the market could bear and to deal with the labour issue on its own. He points out that, in recent decades, the university to a large extent has been supported by three stalwart families: the McCains, the Crawfords, and the Braggs. "Purdy has had his hand on the tiller for a long time, and when he didn't, it was someone very close to him." Even after he left the university's board, Purdy's influence continued. He had been associated with a strong contingent of board members, including Derek Price who headed the important McConnell Foundation; Jim Hankinson, a savvy professional director who once ran Canadian Pacific; and, of course, John Bragg. His oldest daughter Suzanne, a lawyer, joined the board and, as chair in the first decade of the twenty-first century, was instrumental in working with new president Robert Campbell to chart the university's vision for the next quarter century.

Lynn Loewen, a Mount A alumna and financial executive, was working for an airline in Halifax when, in 1997, she got a call from the Toronto office of then-chancellor Purdy Crawford. When they finally met, he said he wanted her on the board, and Loewen agreed to serve. But she had just given birth to a third child, had a big job, and insisted she would not do committees. Good luck. After she joined the board, Purdy was soon on the phone asking her to join a couple of them. She relented and found they were a great introduction to the Mount A network, including the Braggs, the McCains, and Ron Joyce, who had generously supported a new business school. Loewen ultimately became the first woman to chair the board. More than that, she gained two formidable sponsors in Bragg and Crawford. "John is very helpful on the operational side, and with Purdy it is the leadership and mentoring. He points you in a lot of directions."

In recruiting Robert Campbell in 2006, the university's board found an energetic new president whose academic history reflected an appreciation for small universities—he had served as an administrator at Trent University, among other schools. On joining Mount A, he was initiated into the university's community by the Bragg-Crawford tandem with a whirlwind excursion. The three headed out one morning in Bragg's plane and flew to Yarmouth in western Nova Scotia to meet an older alumnus. They then scooted across to eastern Maine to tour Bragg's vast blueberry plantation there. Next, they alighted in Quebec's Eastern Townships for another alumnus visit. Campbell found himself in the Oxford Frozen Foods plant in northern Nova Scotia, at two in the morning, watching the production process. It was a quick education in the public-private world of Mount A: the family business leadership embodied by Bragg and the more corporate, equally passionate guidance of Purdy Crawford.

By this time, the university was back on its feet financially—not a penny of debt—and was highly successful in fundraising, thanks to Chancellor Bragg. But there were demographic perils in the shrinking birth rate in the Maritimes, its home market. "We had an enrollment problem," Campbell says. In the past, the university could hang out its shingle and expect people to come. Now it found that many fewer students from New Brunswick were coming out of high school and going to local universities. All the Maritime schools have great people, great reputations, and great play in social media, but, as Campbell explains, "all we are doing is treading water. We have to recruit outside the region and internationally."

The *Maclean's* rankings helped, but Mount A needed a branding boost. Bragg, Crawford, Campbell, and other backers put their heads together and came up with an out-of-the-box idea. With Bragg leaving the chancellor's role, how about recruiting someone who had little to do with Mount A, no direct link to the Maritimes, and indeed, did not even have a university degree?

What Peter Mansbridge did have was one of the most recognizable faces and voices in Canada. As chief correspondent and anchor for CBC TV, he was the embodiment of this country's TV journalism. In the 1990s he had come to Mount A to give occasional lectures on Canadian public affairs, and in 1999 the university awarded him an honorary degree. He had never met Purdy Crawford before that day, but the two hit it off with talk of politics and public policy. They started getting together back in Toronto for lunch, and the romancing of Peter Mansbridge began.

"We talked about issues of the day and where I was in my career," the TV journalist recalls. "It was about where he thought I could add to my value as a person and professional by doing other things. I was not involved enough in the community outside the CBC." So Mansbridge joined the university's national advisory council, which gave the journalist an education in the challenges of a small university.

Then, in 2009, he got a call from Robert Campbell saying he and Purdy would like to meet with the anchorman. Mansbridge quickly smelled some kind of request. "Whatever the ask was, the odds were I was going to say yes, because it was Purdy." They met at the Osler offices over lunch, and Crawford and Campbell popped the question. Mansbridge was stunned, but it did not take him long to say yes. The potential stumbling block was that he could not, in his CBC correspondent's role, undertake fundraising. But he was told that was not what the university needed from him. It needed someone to carry the flag and make people aware of Mount Allison beyond its normal catchment area.

Some people close to the university were skeptical of the appointment. Mansbridge knew he had to convince them, and he worked hard at dinners, alumni gatherings, and convocations. But the strongest affirmation came from students. Campbell initially had worried that the young undergraduates would not even recognize this conventional TV broadcaster from the public network—their parents' kind of media star. But the moment Mansbridge's beamed-in face hit the screen at the chancellor's unveiling, the place exploded with thunderous applause. For five minutes, Peter Mansbridge's sonorous voice was drowned out by cheers.

Both Bragg and Crawford had been fundraising chancellors, but Mansbridge, who was recently reappointed for a new three-year term ending in 2017, cuts a different figure. He is the brand builder, and he connects with students. He hosts an annual summit which grapples with public policy issues, provides scholarships for global internships, and has given a fine arts prize with his thespian wife Cynthia Dale. And at every graduation, he insists on having a conversation with each student to whom he hands a degree. It is a big event in their lives, he knows. As a young journalist in a hurry, he never had that experience, and it is a regret. Mansbridge's sheer pleasure with the university experience makes him an unconventional success as chancellor and gives Mount Allison added profile—all because Purdy and team were not locked into traditional thinking.

Mount Allison is not the only university where Purdy has left his mark. As Imasco CEO, he became a fundraiser for McGill University, a role that brought him once again in close contact with his good friend, then McGill principal, David Johnston. In a 1999 issue of the *McGill Reporter*, Purdy gave some tips on university fundraising, starting with: don't go into a meeting with a donor alone. "I won't make the call unless I have a professor or a dean—someone closely connected to the project—with me. There are exceptions, but that is how I prefer to do it." In many cases, someone like the director of a particular research body has a passion for why the funds are needed, and that passion comes across more eloquently than if Purdy is doing the talking. Crawford also said in the article that askers have to be aggressive. A McGill development specialist had taught him that "if you go in asking for $10,000, you might well get it, but if you ask for $100,000, you might get $75,000." In later years, Crawford was more nuanced in his approach; in many cases, he would say "we are asking for so much money, but do anything you can." He had learned not to push too hard.

David Johnston asked Purdy to join McGill's board, even though he was still on the board of Mount Allison. The two raised a lot of money, but not without some surprising turns. On one foray, they were going to see a Montrealer who headed a major corporation which had been a donor but not to the degree that reflected its ability. Johnston and Crawford figured they should get $50,000 from a company that had given only $25,000 in the past. They were coached by a fundraising professional who provided a script, in which Crawford would speak for a minute, then Johnston would come in on cue, and the back and forth repartee would proceed apace and captivate the donor.

Totally rehearsed, they entered Mr. Big's office but were forced to wait. For fifteen minutes, they kept thinking of the script and the $50,000 ask. As Johnston recalls, the executive suddenly swept into the office and said "you are a couple of bandits. You're here to squeeze me out of more than I'm inclined to give. I'm going to give you $75,000 and nothing more." Knowing he had a script to get through, Johnston was sputtering to get his words out, until Purdy put his hand over his arm. Crawford said, gently, "the man has made up his mind, and we should let him get back to work to earn that $75,000." Back at the office, the professional asked if they'd used the script. "Didn't get a chance," they admitted. In time, Johnston headed to the University of Waterloo as president and again called on Purdy to accept a board and fundraising role.

Clearly, fundraising style is largely a function of the personality of the fundraiser. Purdy worked a lot with supersalesman Wallace McCain, who was "about the only guy I met who could tell somebody 'that's not enough,' and the other guy wouldn't get mad. Wallace would say 'I don't want to take a cheque for $200,000. I want half a million'."

One of Purdy's McGill forays involved a visit to Bill Mulholland, the outspoken, irascible head of Bank of Montreal in the 1980s. Crawford got into Mulholland's office at the end of a long day for the bank CEO. It was just the two of them. Purdy launched into his pitch and looked up to see Mulholland had fallen sound asleep. "I waited a while and he was still sleeping and I just walked out. He must have been embarrassed because the ultimate gift was more than I anticipated."

Some of his most memorable campaigns were conducted on behalf of Margaret McCain. She recalls going to Imasco to get money for her efforts in the campaign against family violence. "In the 1980s, not many businessmen knew or cared about that issue," Margaret says, but Crawford did, and he was willing to step up with money. He told the Imasco donations committee to listen to this passionate woman from the Maritimes. Any time a fundraising issue came up, she would think of asking Purdy. The most vivid example was when, after she had been established in Toronto, she developed a campaign to build a new national ballet school in the city, and Purdy sat down with her organization to develop a prospects' list. She observes that it is almost an axiom in fundraising that "the same person couldn't go back to the well too many times, but Purdy went back again and again and nobody minded. It wasn't for him but for society, the community. And he never said no to me or Wallace." The tag team of Purdy, Wallace McCain, and Frank McKenna raised $50 million for the ballet school, even though, Margaret says, "you couldn't drag them to a ballet." The approach was: if people don't give, they should, and if they resist, Purdy would call them.

And Crawford's causes have touched a lot of communities. At one point he met Toronto doctor Joseph Wong, founder of the Yee Hong Centres for Geriatric Care, which provide long-term care facilities for Toronto seniors. Crawford became intrigued by the Yee Hong model of community-based nursing homes and support programs. Teaming up with Wong, he helped form the annual Dragon Ball to raise support for the centres. In 2007, he was awarded the Yee Hong Golden Achievement Award, which honours seniors who have made outstanding contributions to Canadian life.

Crawford's role as a tireless fundraiser and donor has been acknowledged in other ways. In 1996, he was made an Officer of the Order of Canada, to honour his standing as "the quintessential corporate philanthropist." The award also noted that, during his career as a lawyer and later as the CEO of one of Canada's largest conglomerates, "he has emerged as a caring and sensitive leader." In May 2007, he was promoted to Companion of the Order, which, in its citation, said "Purdy Crawford's service to the nation is vast and enduring." This time, he was praised for strengthening and developing capital markets in Canada, as well as serving as a volunteer, fundraiser, and mentor. Inducted into the Canadian Business

Hall of Fame, he was cited as someone "known for his integrity and commitment to worthy causes."

The other side of the coin is that the boy from Five Islands had become a wealthy man and someone whose wise counsel was asked for when people wanted to accumulate wealth, as well as give it away. He earned the reputation as a kind of northern Warren Buffett— particularly fitting, because Buffett is his hero, and both have been successful in that contrarian task of building successful conglomerates, deploying the same basic principles: invest in what you know and act like an owner, not just a paper flipper.

Purdy relishes the great game of investing: the hunt for value and the payoff when a stock pans out. He started buying stocks sixty years ago, and he has been quietly, sagely successful ever since. He has never shied away from debt, but he has never been what he considers over-leveraged—too much debt for his own good.

Soon after joining Osler, he was able to borrow to buy shares. "I arranged to borrow some money from the TD bank, where Osler banked in those days. It seemed like a lot but it was only $15,000." He was given special consideration to bypass the bank's required collateral coverage. "Normally, if you wanted to invest $75,000, you needed coverage for $100,000. But they let me go one-for-one: if I had $15,000, I could borrow $15,000 for securities." For his investment decision making, he originally used one or two investment brokers for advice, but, he notes with some delight, "later they came to rely on me, and it was the start of the process."

Purdy not only admired Warren Buffett and his rules of long-term-value investing; he also made a modest investment in the Omaha sage's Berkshire Hathaway holding company, buying shares in the late 1970s. Almost forty years later, his Berkshire holdings were worth $5 million. But his biggest coup was the result of another Buffett rule: buy what you know. He took that chance on Genstar Development, the property development company spun out of Imasco, which has grown mightily based on its land holdings in Canada and the United States. He shouldered a lot of debt to buy Genstar shares and, as described in an earlier chapter, was joined by the Sobey family and their holding company, Empire.

David and Donald Sobey are no second raters themselves. They are both savvy about markets, as was their late father Frank, another legendary investor. They admit they get interested in a company if they know Purdy is involved, because they feel he would do the best job possible for shareholders. David Sobey remembers that, when Crawford joined the board of CN, the company started to change and grow in its new privatized form. "I started to buy shares, and I sure wish I had bought more. Purdy is something like Buffett. I think his influence was pretty positive." He also saw the Purdy effect when the Sobey family bought into Domtex, which was reeling from a frustrating pattern of stock-funded acquisitions, followed by share-price declines. In the end, David says, as Domtex declined and was sold off, Crawford was valuable in getting shareholders out for more than they invested. "I got more out than I put in, and I think people like Purdy helped."

Domtex was a frustrating experience because it had strong management but was locked in a tough business and trade environment. Donald Sobey quotes Warren Buffett on that issue as well: "When you have good management in a bad business, it is the business that will maintain its reputation." Like Buffett he adds that, as an investor, you have to think, "I own a piece of that business." That is Purdy's credo, as well.

For several years in the mid-1990s, Donald Sobey organized a pilgrimage to the annual meetings of Berkshire Hathaway in Buffett's hometown of Omaha. These are heavily attended events, with thousands of Buffett worshippers in attendance. Donald would bring along Purdy, as well as John Bragg. Flying on a private plane, the group always added an extra trip to the excursion. One year, they took a side trip to Mount Rushmore to see the American political legends etched in stone. It was the perfect trip for Crawford, for he is a student not just of Buffett but of American history.

Purdy's philosophy is that a good investor is a good business-man, and a good businessman will be a good investor. When he invests, he is betting on good managers, whether it is Paul Tellier or Hunter Harrison at Canadian National—which in later life was still his biggest holding, valued at the end of 2013 at $18 million. And he has been putting his money on the people he knows at TD Bank, his second-highest holding with more than $10 million worth of shares. He is not a big technology investor, but in late 2013 he was holding a lot of CGI, the Canadian computer solutions giant. Despite its unfortunate role in the clumsy rollout of Obamacare, Purdy knows and respects the top managers.

He once told journalist Amanda Lang in an article for *Report on Business* magazine that he makes investments based on a range of macroeconomic information, industry fundamentals, business-specific data, and, most important, his judgment of management. "I don't do mathematics or how much you get when you multiply operating earnings by whatever. I rely very much on what I think about people who operate the company. And I read a lot." In 2013, for example, he had read a lot about the Quebec-based convenience store operator Couche-Tard, and he had been stocking up on its shares. "The guy who runs it was CEO of the Year, and it is a good organization. You always wonder when it might stop growing. But they've got a moat, as Buffett would say, against the competition."

In late 2013, he saw Manulife as a buy after he had watched its top management guide the company through hell in the wake of the financial meltdown. And, of course, he respects the CEO, Donald Guloien. Another company on its way back was the US conglomerate General Electric. He had owned GE when it was run by longtime CEO Jack Welch. "I knew Welch, and I always felt the company would go to hell [after him]," but in recent times Welch's successor Jeff Immelt has been showing his mettle.

Purdy's other rule is that, to acquire wealth, investors have to take on risk—but not too much. He always admonishes lawyers because they tend to be ultra-cautious to the point of paralysis. "Their idea of debt is: don't do that. I used to lecture them and say you finish practising law and you have a pension, but you are not going to have accumulated significant wealth." By taking some measured risks, Purdy did accumulate significant personal wealth.

Genstar's president, Frank Thomas, says Crawford, both as a CEO and an investor, is a connoisseur of good management. Purdy stretched to buy an interest in his company, but he has profited from the year-after-year success. One Christmas, Thomas got a card from Purdy that said, "Frank, you're my favourite executive." Genstar "made me rich," Purdy says, then adds, with the knowing smile of someone who advises billionaires, "it depends what you mean by rich."

## Chapter Eleven

# MARKET MAYHEM

F rancesca Guolo had a blissful maternity leave. It was not just because of the arrival of her new baby daughter, but also a four-month break from the hectic life of a Bay Street lawyer with the top-tier firm Goodmans. During the last month, as she relaxed in Ontario cottage country, things were getting rough out in her field of practice, the world of derivatives, hedge funds, and structured finance. The collapse of the US housing market had infected markets, and trading in a whole class of structured products had simply frozen. "Wow, that's not good," she thought from the rented cottage in Haliburton. Even so, she came back refreshed and recharged the day after Labour Day 2007. Her office desk sat there uncluttered, like an empty canvas waiting for a splash of colour.

But not for long. Her colleague Steve Halperin invited her to his office and, with wry understatement, said there was this "interesting little file" in which she might want to be involved. She took a look at the assignment and her jaw dropped. "I knew it had the potential to be massive, and it would be challenging. I said, 'I can't believe you described this as interesting and little, all in the same sentence'."

She learned that Goodmans had won the job to provide the legal advice on the biggest financial restructuring in Canadian history: the fight to salvage the market in third-party (or non-bank) asset-backed commercial paper. It sounded arcane and it was, but it was also big:

$35 billion of investments sitting in limbo with repercussions that touched every Canadian.

It was a market she understood but few others did. The world of structured products was almost a cult, a kind of inside game that the investment community tolerated because it made them a whole lot of money. It would consume Guolo for the next eighteen months, disrupt her family life and her sleep, and throw her into phone calls at all hours, dealing with hurt, frightened, angry people. But she would get to work with a legend, Bay Street's most respected figure. Her initial challenge was the education of Purdy Crawford. If he were to save this market—perhaps save all Canadian markets—from chaos, he had to understand it.

"The reality is I didn't have a clue what the hell it was about," says Purdy, looking back on the summer of 2007. As a lawyer, he was grounded in the real world of mergers and takeovers, but these investments were artificial, manufactured—in fact, engineered. "We started with the driving principles," Guolo said, "but once he understood the basics, Purdy said, 'Okay, I get where the economics lie, where the motivations are, I get what we need to do'."

He knew he had to depend on specialists like Guolo to fill in the technical details and processes while he managed the big picture. Guolo and her colleague Gale Rubenstein were two more in a long line of brilliant women whose minds he tapped and whose careers he would touch in a positive way. This project was not Purdy acting as a lawyer or a securities expert who had drafted the law. He was here as mediator, cajoler, networker, a rock of stability and sanity—and the amiable, unbending hub in a massive rescue operation. It turned out to be his finest hour, although he terribly misjudged the toll it would take. Sitting in his office, in late August 2007, Purdy figured he'd be back to normal life by Christmas. He just didn't anticipate which Christmas, or that he would spend two Christmas Eves in committee meetings before the crisis would grind to a conclusion.

And he was absolutely the right person to take it on, says his protegé Brian Levitt. "He is very smart, for starters. It takes a certain mind to understand that stuff. You can hire all the advisors you want, and they have to give inputs, but you have to know it." And, he adds, it is not just about being smarter—"the differentiator is how hard people work; there is no substitute for work." And Purdy, even at seventy-five, was a horse for work.

The trigger for this assignment was the bursting of the US housing bubble, an insane boom built on the rickety foundation of dubious sub-prime mortgages issued to homebuyers with low credit ratings. Sharp operators in the financial industry packaged these shaky mortgages with good mortgages, car loans, credit card receivables, and other debts of varying quality into investment pools they could sell to the public. Despite the mix of bad and good assets, compliant bond-rating agencies labelled them as triple-A securities that even a retired person could buy safely. They were the building blocks of a breed of investment instruments called third-party asset-backed commercial paper (ABCP). They were advertised as safe, short-term notes that paid more than traditional alternatives such as treasury bills. Why third party? The banks had their own commercial paper, which came with their own cash guarantees. This was a different beast, a stew of assets compiled in special-purpose entities called conduits. Some financial institutions did agree to back them with cash guarantees but only, it turned out, if the world went to hell in a handbasket. It hadn't done that—yet.

And here's the rub. If the market were liquidated, it would be a nightmare. The vast majority of these pools were not really backed by assets, as mortgages or credit card debt were. Instead, they consisted of derivative products called credit default swaps—basically insurance policies against "a credit event": a massive inability to pay debt. The swaps were highly leveraged—there was much more insurance out there than collateral. In the case of a disastrous credit event, a shift in mathematical ratios on a computer screen could trigger a cascade of calls for collateral. At a leverage ratio of eight to ten or even twenty to one, a $35 billion problem could easily balloon to $300 billion in margin calls rippling through the economy. (It would soon be reduced to a $32 billion problem when some of the paper, with more transparent assets, was hived off in separate trusts.)

And the products were like Russian nesting dolls: take off one layer and you uncap a series of more obligations and more triggers. Who knew what the economic impact would be? It showed the extent, in the early twenty-first century, to which a coterie of mathematical geniuses had put entire economies at risk, emboldened by greedy financiers, indifferent credit rating agencies, and hapless regulators.

Then the worst happened. As the housing bubble burst, it triggered a tsunami of mortgage defaults, a massive erosion of phony asset values and wealth that triggered the Great Recession. Canada's ABCP crisis was the dress rehearsal for the market meltdown. In fact, an estimated 7 percent of the third-party ABCP market was devoted to sub-prime mortgages, but this little fact was lost in the opaque structure of the conduits. The lack of transparency meant the house of cards collapsed in a heap. Any whiff of toxic mortgages was anathema to scared-stiff investors.

The assets and liabilities packaged in these conduits had a mess of varying maturities, and yet people bought them as short-term parking places for money. The market worked like a constantly moving carousel: when one person stepped off, another would step on. Whenever a note was sold for cash, there was always someone stepping up to buy—or new notes were constantly being issued to pay off the sellers. That carousel stopped on August 13, 2007: no more buyers, no issuers, no market. Nothing would roll over.

The paralysis touched just about everyone in Canada's financial community, from bankers who sold the stuff, to bankers who held the guarantees, who were often the same people, and a Who's Who of investors, including the massive Caisse de dépôt et placement du Québec, which held more than $13 billion of the notes, and players such as the federal Public Service Pension Plan, Alberta's government-owned ATB Financial, and National Bank, which were all into it for a billion or more. The Greater Toronto Airport Authority had almost $250 million of the stuff, the city of Hamilton $10 million, and various mining companies held the notes to fund new mines and exploration ventures.

Thus, the market collapse threatened to leave a big hole in the personal finances of Canadians. It would hit major pension funds, in some cases hurting their ability to meet the rising crescendo of obligations. But there was also a direct personal cost, which was un-appreciated early in the game. About 1,800 ordinary investors, some with a million dollars or more at risk, but many with much less—cash earmarked for retirement, a grandchild's education, proceeds from selling one house to buy another—now saw their investments become worthless, unless the market could be restructured.

The worry went to the top levels of government, to Finance Minister Jim Flaherty, to Bank of Canada governor David Dodge, and to his deputy, Mark Carney, who would replace Dodge on the first day of 2008. They all saw the potential ripples—and how the crisis would be a black mark on Canada's reputation for stellar financial management. But they were also determined it would not be met with a public bailout, but as a private sector restructuring. Bailing out the market with government funding would send a bad message. If you invest in some instrument and things go terribly wrong, you shouldn't expect government to be there as a backstop. The problem was that nobody had ever successfully restructured a market of this size. It would make history, bad or good. "We were making stuff up from a legal standpoint up as we went along," Steve Halperin says.

One of the few financial chiefs with little at stake in the game was TD Bank's Ed Clark. His bank did not sell the third-party, non-TD ABCP.

Clark's view was "would I sell it to my mother-in-law? No, I wouldn't. So why should I sell it to customers?" It was voodoo, he liked to say. But the sale of third-party ABCP was so widespread that Clark and his bank would not escape the impact if the collapse of that market infected the entire economy.

On the day the market ground to a halt, Coventree—the biggest player in the market—announced it could not sell its new ABCP notes, citing "unfavorable market conditions" resulting from the US sub-prime mortgage crisis. Coventree said some of its ABCP trusts were refused emergency funding from liquidity providers. That money would be freed only in the event of a widespread market disruption in all forms of ABCP, and technically that was not happening.

Something had to be done. The response came three days later, on August 16, when ten market players met in Montreal and proposed to freeze the ABCP market for sixty days and cast around for a solution. This Montreal Accord was signed by financial players with a strong Quebec Inc. flavour: pension fund managers such as the Caisse de dépôt, financial institutions such as Desjardins Group and National Bank, plus a smattering of foreign banks, including German giant Deutsche Bank and US powerhouse Merrill Lynch.

Unlike Ed Clark and TD Bank, the Caisse did have a lot riding on the outcome. Not only was it the biggest ABCP holder; it was also a co-creator of the market as a founding shareholder in Coventree. Its big-personality CEO, Henri-Paul Rousseau, would become, after Purdy Crawford, the most important player in the saga. It was he who made the call to the Toronto lawyer in that fateful week leading up to Labour Day, with the backing of the federal government and the Bank of Canada. Purdy knew the burly Rousseau and also knew he could be a polarizing force in the industry, but he felt he could work with him: "Whether you like him or not, he's a leader." Purdy told Rousseau he would take a few days to think about it. The rule: always spend at least a night sleeping on a big decision.

That phone call also signalled a shift in the action from Montreal to Toronto, and beyond the universe of Quebec Inc. The background players felt Purdy was perhaps the only person in Canada with the experience, prestige, and contacts to pull off a rescue. But he also represented the new reality that it had become a national challenge, rather than just a Quebec problem.

Purdy was leaning toward saying yes, but he needed a capable legal team. Osler had a conflict of interest—indeed, most of the major law firms were already lining up behind the corporate players in the drama. Purdy thought about Goodmans and Steve Halperin—the two men had sat together on the board of AT&T Canada, a telecom firm that had to be restructured in 2002–2003. Halperin was a congenial guy in his late fifties, with a warm smile and a sharp mind honed over thirty years of representing such clients as mining tycoon Robert Friedland. He and his colleagues knew the issues first-hand—they had clients whose deals were stuck in the deep freeze of the market—but, from a combination of luck and planning, the firm had kept its entanglements to a minimum, hoping for a more central role in solving the crisis.

On the Thursday before Labour Day, Crawford asked Halperin if he had any involvement with the main players. He said there was nothing major, so Purdy invited him to a key meeting with the investor committee the day after Labour Day. "If I do take it on, I'd like you to be my counsel," Crawford said. On September 6, 2007, a press release confirmed that a pan-Canadian committee chaired by Crawford had been formed to oversee the proposed restructuring of the third-party ABCP. The press release was shaded in nuance. Purdy had asked for a rewrite to reflect the attention he would give to all investors, not just the heavyweights. It reflected a tension that would play out over the next eighteen months: the need to save the system versus the need to pay out small investors. Purdy knew then they were twin priorities. For the first goal to succeed, he had to carry everyone with him.

Right from the beginning, Sue Lucas, his administrative assistant, could see the toll it would take. With his role now official and
Goodmans on board, Crawford retired to his Caledon country house
for a restorative weekend, only to be bombarded with phone calls. "It
was all-consuming—at least I got the weekends off," Lucas said. Not
Purdy. On a typical Monday morning, after a weekend of constant
messaging, she would run off three hundred pages of emails he had
received. Then there was a barrage of phone calls. It was enough to
break down his Luddite tendencies. He would sit in meetings and
watch Steve Halperin work his BlackBerry, and he didn't want to be
left behind. "He is one of the most unsavvy tech persons in the world,
and he even got a BlackBerry," Lucas marvels.

Next up was the hiring of a financial adviser. There were a number
of Canadian and US applicants, but it narrowed down to two US investment banking giants, JP Morgan and Lehman Brothers, both highly
qualified and lacking conflicts. The committee ended up picking JP
Morgan, and it unwittingly dodged a big bullet—Lehman Brothers'
collapse a year later could have scuttled the entire deal.

The hiring of JP Morgan drew another important figure into the
saga: banker Andrew Kresse, a thirty-five-year-old derivatives hotshot
who grew up in Buffalo, just down the highway from Toronto, and
who laboured on Wall Street. He would make an improbable team
with Purdy. Kresse was brilliant on financial instruments, but he also
had a gift for reducing things to their basic essence. That was valuable,
as JP Morgan had to explain the market to stakeholders, including
governments at all levels. One player recalls Kresse's team coming to
see him and leading him through the maze of swaps, triggers, and
margin calls. Even someone with a PhD in economics had trouble
peeling the onion and finding the hard core of the matter.

As the committee proceeded through the fall of 2007, it became
clear this was no four-month wonder. There were pitched battles
among interests who didn't want to give an inch. The struggle

between foreign banks and domestic banks took up a lot of time, and economic explosions were being set off in the rest of the world. As well, Purdy had to manage the larger-than-life egos at the table. He is normally skilled at finding the good in all people and working with it, but even he inwardly seethed at those who blocked the process unnecessarily—who would not budge if it meant compromising their narrow interests. Instead, he often found common ground with a second-in-command who might grasp the bigger picture.

The goal was to structure a new set of instruments to replace the frozen ABCP notes, and that meant consolidating the market into a small number of pools. The committee would create a new class of securities with matching maturities and with crystal-clear transparency in terms of the asset mix. The idea was if these notes were held to maturity, investors could get out with full payback. For those not able to wait, the capital they would get back would not make them whole, but it would be more than if there were a forced liquidation.

But it was clear very early that the players would agree to a restructuring only if they could obtain assurance that they would not be sued. The turning point, some said, came in a meeting with foreign banks. There was an element of despair over whether they could bridge the gap between interests—until someone mentioned the releases from litigation. "No one wanted to admit the releases were that important, but it had become a driver," says one observer. And it also became apparent that something called CCAA was the vehicle to make it all happen.

And what exactly is CCAA? It is the abbreviation for a piece of legislation known as the Companies' Creditors Arrangement Act, a device commonly used by financially troubled companies to buy time and reorganize without facing bankruptcy. The act had become a mainstay of the Canadian insolvency system and had made a lot of money for lawyers and accountants. The decision to file for CCAA was a defining moment, because this was not a company—it was not

Allstream or Bramalea or Olympia & York, but an entire industry or, more precisely, an entire market. This had never been done before.

Things would unroll through the fall, as the Montreal Accord kept getting extended. But the issue was still only on the fringe of most people's minds. A reality check came in mid-December, when David Dodge, set to retire as Bank of Canada governor at the end of the month, visited the *National Post* editorial board and warned that all Canadians could pay a price if banks failed to come up with an agreement to save the ABCP market. "If the whole market goes into a shambles everybody gets affected, including Mr. and Mrs. Jones on Main Street," said Dodge. Because of the leverage factor, "the amount of global assets that would be affected if all this went down would be eight or ten times the nominal value of the notes, so you're starting to get into the $200 billion, quarter-trillion dollars' worth." The proposed bailout obviously would still involve losses, he said, but if the market did come back over time, those losses would be "cents on the dollar or nickels on the dollar and not dimes and quarters on the dollar."

One encouraging note was that, on December 20, 2007, one part of the market that had been spun off, the $2 billion Skeena Capital Trust, was successfully restructured. And on December 23, the Crawford committee said it expected to complete the final proposal by mid-March.

In the waning hours of the year, Goodmans brought one of their best insolvency lawyers into the mix. Gale Rubenstein, a veteran of the bankruptcy wars, is a mix of toughness and quick wit, and she became the key insolvency person on the file—and a close confidante of Purdy's. She admits the thought of working with him was intimidating. "I started off scared," she says. The talk was all "Purdy, Purdy, Purdy." But like many who have been awed by the reputation, she found the reality far less daunting. "He was a little bit of a flirt, which I enjoyed tremendously—and funny. He was wonderful and incredibly respectful. It takes a lot to be under that kind of pressure; he never lost it." And by the time she arrived, the route seemed clear: "Everybody felt the only way to implement it was through CCAA."

When Rubenstein went to her first meeting at the Goodmans offices, then located at 250 Yonge Street, she encountered a scene that looked like a legislature of a small republic. The meetings would swell to fifty or more people, necessitating a microphone and speakers to keep everyone informed. Or it might be compared to a family meal, where the adults met at the big table and there were kids' tables along the sides. Room had to be made not just for the major investors, but also for their squads of lawyers. At first, Purdy tried to limit the lawyers to one per investor around the table, but that quickly broke down. Soon, Goodmans was renting more space.

Members of the investor committee sat around the big table and in the middle of that, flanked by Halperin and Jim Riley, the two senior Goodmans lawyers on the case, there sat this heavy-set man who kept things moving forward. People would be called to the mic and give their bit, and Purdy nudged them to be as brief as possible.

"Boy, did they pick the right guy!" thought one observer, Benita Warmbold, the CFO of Northwater Capital, a company that not only invested in ABCP but also had expertise that Purdy could tap on the committee. "To watch him in those meetings, he would manage all the personalities in the room. He was a master. He made sure everyone heard and understood." And not far away was Andrew Kresse, who, Warmbold says, "put his heart and soul into this." (Warmbold would later become the chief financial officer of the Canada Pension Plan Investment Board.)

And Purdy had to keep all the government players informed. The Department of Finance had a top Toronto lawyer, Gar Emerson, monitoring the hearings, but Minister Jim Flaherty gave Purdy his cell phone number—and he would take a call any place, any time. Purdy did not know Flaherty well before the ABCP debacle and did not always agree with him politically, but came to admire his ability to manage a crisis. Purdy remembers an emergency phone call to Flaherty as the minister was being driven into Vancouver. The car was immediately commanded off to the side, as Flaherty quickly dealt with the issue. Such a response was typical of Flaherty and other players, who took time off from sessions in Brazil, Brussels, New York—just to answer Purdy. "I had the heads of Canadian banks and their direct lines, and I got along pretty well with them," he says.

The Goodmans crew was growing into a massive team, with dozens of lawyers involved in some way. Francesca Guolo's own crew consisted of thirty to forty full-time people and others coming in for bits and pieces. The restructuring would cost more than $200 million in total fees, and that doesn't begin to describe the cost to all the players. In a time of financial stress, it was a goldmine for lawyers—although nothing on the scale of similar reorganizations in the United States.

Until then, Crawford had never been paid anything for his public service, but this time he got $40,000 a month, and he wryly observes that he probably could have asked for and got $100,000—it was that important a file, with $32 billion of frozen assets. He had always felt in corporate reorganizations that the lawyers shouldn't shoot for the moon but should leave some fees on the table to help the company revive. But he was amazed at the money tossed around this time.

And, according to David Johnston, it required a special kind of person to pull it off: "It was knowledge of the law but also an extraordinary exercise of personality to hold that loose coalition together." He had to tell them to "hold off on trying to cash in your dollars because you will bring the whole thing down. If you are just prepared to be patient, our system will come out of this." And Purdy, he says, was no spring chicken. That kind of resolution would not have happened in the United States, Johnston argues, and if it happened in the United Kingdom, it would be behind closed doors. "It was kind of an open, town-hall democracy that pulled it off."

But it also required a lot of private arm twisting. New Year 2008 passed with no resolution, and the team was aiming for a March approval of the restructuring plan. One key condition was that the Canadian banks had to come up with money to backstop the new notes and their collateral guarantees, and some of them were balking. Scotiabank was complaining about the sums, and Royal Bank was not keen, especially if TD was not in—and TD was obdurate.

"We were in a different position than anyone else," Ed Clark recalls. It had been a difficult decision to abstain from selling third-party ABCP, depriving his sales force of a product everyone else sold. Then, when it all came crashing down, and Purdy was in charge of the rescue, Clark was still thinking, "why should I help bail out a bunch of guys who did a stupid thing? That is not a good message." Purdy kept approaching Clark, and the banker would say no, he wouldn't do it. Crawford would nod his head and go back to work. Purdy told Clark he thought he could achieve what he wanted without him—but there might be a point when he would have to come back for help.

Then, in early 2008, the rescue was coming to a make-or-break moment, when the participation of the other banks depended on having everyone in. Purdy told Clark he needed TD's backing, and Clark agreed to pitch in $50 million. In the final analysis, says Clark, "I'm a Canadian citizen before I am the CEO of TD Bank, and you are not doing this for yourself." TD's contribution, after all, was part of the effort to help save the country. The Bank of Canada felt that way too—new governor Mark Carney was making a strong push, feeling it needed the full-frontal Canadian approach. So the TD came in, and Royal as well.

Even with the major financial players on board, it was far from over. All hell was breaking loose in the world beyond Canadian finance. In the United States in mid-March, with $30 billion in public bailout money and under pressure from regulators, the teetering investment bank Bear Stearns signed a rescue merger agreement with JP Morgan Chase.

It was a signal of the gathering financial calamity, and a huge blow to the ABCP committee because it came at the worst possible time—on the eve of filing the restructuring plan with an Ontario judge. Everyone was watching the screens for the latest interest rate spreads that would apply to the proposed instruments—as if they had been already issued—and suddenly they were widening. The spreads had to be tight to avoid triggering a collateral call, but now the comfort level for issuing the proposed notes was disappearing.

Purdy and his team were at a Toronto courthouse on a Friday afternoon to file their application for CCAA. Back at Goodmans, Gale Rubenstein was applying the last touches. Then Henri-Paul Rousseau called at the last moment and said the ratios had deteriorated so badly they had to look at the filing again—and that included the affidavit that Purdy was about to submit under his own name, a piece of carefully worded prose that explained why this route was being taken and how it would unfold. The team pulled back the filing and renegotiated over the weekend. "There were 90 gazillion drafts," Rubenstein recalls, and through it all "Purdy was completely wonderful; he was reading things all the time. He was very concerned about the tone."

Crawford's affidavit had gone from firm certainty to cautious hedging, especially around the idea of a secondary market in these new notes. The final wording: "It is expected that investors who do not wish to hold the restructured notes until maturity will be able to trade their restructured notes when markets stabilize." The key words were "it is expected" and "when markets stabilize." His caution was driven by a market that had turned ugly. By the time the investors voted, markets had stabilized, but who knew at the time?

The affidavit also contained a plea to release the financial players from future lawsuits. It was absolutely necessary for the plan to happen, but it was a hard sell to badly burned investors. "Some investors would believe their rights were taken away," the affidavit conceded. But, in classic Crawfordian words, it argued that negotiation of the

168

plan had been the art of the possible: "Key participants who are making a substantial and necessary contribution required the releases. Simply put, there can be no plan unless these releases are included, and I believe that the benefits of the plan, taken as a whole, justify the releases." The end, in short, justified a rather imperfect means.

On March 17, 2008, Ontario Superior Court Justice Colin Campbell granted bankruptcy protection to twenty ABCP trusts, conditional on a vote by investors. And that vote was still uncertain. Purdy had known for some time about the added wrinkle—under CCAA rules, such a plan would have to be approved by a double majority. There had to be a two-thirds majority of the principal invested—and the big investors such as the Caisse de dépôt were on board, so that should be easy—but it also had to be approved by a majority of investors, and under those terms Henri-Paul Rousseau, with $13 billion, had the same single vote as an RRSP holder in Alberta with $10,000.

The reality was that 1,800 or so small investors had the power to kill the deal, perhaps setting off at least another decade of lawsuits and untold costs to Canada. Purdy thought he could pull it off, but he didn't realize how hard that would be. Until now, he had been dealing with the massive egos and fragile finances of the big players. In the next phase, he would have to deal with a whole new cast of unpredictable characters.

## Chapter Twelve

# THE ART OF THE POSSIBLE

B rian Hunter is a Calgary oil man who exudes a potent mix of charm and blasphemous irreverence. He describes the week of August 13, 2007, as his "WTF moment"— a popular short form of an expletive that captures the shock when something hits you out of the blue. It was when he learned that half his RRSP—a total of $650,000, which the fifty-five-year-old had been saving for retirement—had fallen into a big dark hole. The funds were frozen in the ABCP debacle.

It wasn't supposed to be this way. He had withdrawn funds from a supposedly risky investment and put them into what he thought were ultra-safe notes—and he could get the cash when he wanted. Then the market froze. Friends told him it likely would be solved in a week, but it wasn't. The investments had looked on the surface to be sound enough—car loans, credit card receivables, and other real assets—but "nobody knew it was completely synthetic," Hunter recalls bitterly. "There was really no product. A few percent of it was real stuff, but the rest of it was notional."

There were a lot of people cursing just as creatively as Brian Hunter, including corporate players that had parked money earmarked for investment, building mines, and paying off loans. It was a cross-section of Canadian business, from Barrick Gold to Empire, the holding company for the Sobeys' grocery and real estate assets. But the saddest stories could be found among the small retail investors whose brokers and financial planners had poured them into this allegedly safe vessel. The big investors had their lawyers; the small investors had Brian Hunter, who was suddenly thrust centre stage as an advocate for the ordinary man, a social media revolutionary, and, most surprisingly, a partner with Purdy Crawford on his mission to prevent a catastrophe.

The relationship did not start well. Hunter had sent letters to the Crawford committee and didn't get much response. "To begin with, I unkindly said, 'there is this seventy-five-year-old guy there—is he senile? Are they using him as a front?' I got a patronizing response written probably by other people." He communicated with the Bank of Canada, asking why Mark Carney and company could bail out Canadian banks and do nothing for small investors—and again got no satisfaction. "The whole thing stank. And yet this is a significant part of my assets—half of what I had in RRSPs. Hell, you've been working a twenty-five-year career and that's the pension."

He figured the best weapon was press attention, and he started talking to reporters Boyd Erman of the *Globe and Mail* and Jim Middlemiss of the *National Post*. They found it all interesting, and he got some coverage. Then, one day, someone at his broker's firm, Canaccord Genuity, by mistake included him in an email with a "cc" list of other investors. He now had twenty-one email addresses. Suddenly, he wasn't alone—he was a movement.

Hunter had used Facebook to keep in touch with his kids away at college by trading pictures and messages. Then he hit upon the idea that it could be a forum for folks in the same ABCP rut. The social media campaign was successful in ways he didn't anticipate. It changed the image of the small investor group by capturing the imagination of the press. They were no longer thought of as stupid people who had put money in bad investments, but enterprising and cutting edge.

He jokes that, to begin, he had ten guys signed up on Facebook, and half of them were his actual friends. But with more and more contacts, the movement snowballed, and there were now hundreds.

Meanwhile, Purdy Crawford was grappling with the reality of the double majority and the fact that the deal depended on the support of this inchoate group for which Hunter had become the unofficial spokesman and Facebook its rallying point. Crawford felt he had to go on the road to talk to the retail investors, get their input, and reassure them that a solution was at hand. Brian Hunter saw that as his opportunity, as well. He and his fellow travellers organized across the country in advance of the vote—so that it would look like a mass movement, even if it were something less than that.

There were not many ABCP investors in Atlantic Canada, so no meetings would be held there, but the road show would travel in late March and early April to Montreal and Toronto in the East and Edmonton, Calgary, and Vancouver in the West. The first meetings in Montreal and Toronto were spirited but not out of control. The Calgary crowd was pretty much all business, and Hunter showed up, taking time to meet Purdy for the first time. "He was very respectful and we had a nice chat," the oilman recalled. Hunter's parting words to Purdy were: "Enjoy yourself in Vancouver." He knew that Vancouver would host the biggest contingent of ordinary retail investors, and it would be a circus.

But his opinion of Purdy was starting to change. "I thought initially that this was some old guy who was up here because he could be easily controlled by the banks, just a pretty face. But I found that he was really smart and hadn't lost too many steps, and there was some pretty good horsepower working closely with him saying, how do you solve this?"

Some of that horsepower, in the form of Andrew Kresse, the key JP Morgan advisor, Adam Howard, then CEO of JP Morgan in Canada, and Steve Halperin of Goodmans, accompanied Purdy on the road trip. They watched as Purdy, suffering from various ailments, moved from city to city. "There were times I worried as we travelled," Halperin says. David Crawford, Purdy's son and a Toronto compensation consultant, said, "we were all very concerned about his health and the whole mental strain." Sister Heather, a lawyer, would make phone calls in advance of the meetings, making sure there was a railing to support him and a chair with arms.

Hunter was right in guessing the Vancouver meeting would be a circus. The West Coast was the home of Canaccord Genuity, which, along with the credit union movement, had been the most active in selling ABCP products to retail investors. It was a hotbed of angry, frightened people, and the public meeting, with Purdy in the centre, became the focus of their anger. The meeting attracted several hundred people to the Sutton Place Hotel, and Purdy took a barrage of criticism for over two hours.

Some of the committee advisors were aghast at what looked like a public lynching. They sensed that by this time Purdy had a plan to make sure these investors could be made whole. He knew the double majority was the linchpin of the reorganization. According to some, he knew as early as September 2007 that retail investors would carry the day. But he did not betray his game plan until he had the rest of his committee with him. He wanted to take them to the brink and then pull back and say "this is what we have to do. We have to bail out the little guys."

Meanwhile, he was a punching bag for people with varying agendas—some to punish the banks and the brokers, others to change or overthrow the system, and many just to make money off the picked-over carcass of the ABCP market. He was taking a huge hit on the Internet and now in person. One person close to the committee observed that "people had no idea of these products, should never have been sold them, and they had to yell at somebody and we were the only people to yell at. Purdy was most upset about it." And now there was the added insult of not being able to sue the alleged villains.

In Vancouver, reporter Tara Perkins of the *Globe and Mail* noted in her news report that Purdy kept his cool most of the day. But his breaking point appeared to come as Bill Galine, executive vice-president of Universal Uranium Ltd., with $1.4 million of ABCP investments, posed several pointed questions, including, "Who is going to jail here?" Galine asked him why financial institutions shouldn't have to take care of retail investors, "the ones who are desperate and put their money in and didn't know the deal. Is that fair?" Purdy answered back, raising his voice: "That's what I've been trying to tell you all day, that that's what's going to happen." He explained: "I think there's sunshine over the hill for you. I assure you we will try to make sure the sun shines."

Purdy was frustrated but not entirely discouraged. "Vancouver was the most difficult [meeting]—[there] they had probably the most small investors. But a lot of them came away feeling different, that we were part of the solution, not the problem." It also brought the committee face to face with the human cost of the ABCP debacle. Steve Halperin was exposed to "a lot of very sad stories of people who couldn't send kids to university, a lot of pensioners. It redoubled [Purdy's] desire that small investors be looked after." One woman said she was on the verge of suicide. Purdy would spend long periods on the phone with her, trying to reassure that she would come out whole, and she weathered it.

Brian Hunter would pass these difficult cases on to Purdy. "I'm just a dumb engineer and not qualified to do social work. I think he had empathy, and a lot of people had their life's savings in this." Hunter realized he was one of the youngest people affected—the average age was about sixty-five, he figures. He shakes his head to think of the small investors who bought these products from credit unions. "I was still working, but others were eighty, ninety years old. There were stories of cancer—every sad story." Hunter, meanwhile, was simply "an oilman who made a bad investment, you dumb ass.

That is just the way it is when investments go bad. But this was so egregious it was worthy of taking a run at it." And so he kept up the pressure on Purdy, and Purdy brought him into his tent.

The first committee meeting back in Toronto was dramatic. Rousseau rose to thank Purdy and his team for undertaking the road show. They clearly had taken a hit for the team, standing up to hours of abuse. Even before the road trip, there was a sense that the small investors would have to be bailed out, but now it was urgent. "If there was any question there had to be a deal, it became readily apparent then," says one lawyer. "You were not dealing with a group prepared to come to the table and negotiate. There was profound disappointment—you knew it, but you didn't know it was that bad."

But the bailout would have to be accomplished outside the committee, in confidential side deals. Everyone with up to $1 million invested would be paid off in full. Again, it was not perfect. And it was controversial: a lot of small players would still be hurt, because, in terms of retirement income, a million dollars is no longer a rich bounty; many middle-class people see it as the bare minimum needed to retire. There were also scores of small corporate holders, such as the mining firms. At least one company would go under, lacking access to its cash. And any payouts would have to wait until the whole deal got done.

Now, Brian Hunter was practically part of the team, keeping communication lines open to investors. He was on the phone for weekly updates with Purdy and Gale Rubenstein. He became, in Purdy's mind, an unofficial member of the investors' committee. Hunter, who had first disparaged Crawford, was now convinced "he was absolutely the right guy. It was a difficult project but he had the stature." He noted that there was a determined group that saw Purdy as a whipping boy, and they lashed at him for his board memberships, his elite law firm stature, and his experience in the tobacco industry. But Hunter just wanted his money, and he came to feel Purdy could achieve that. Crawford's decision to spend time with him was smart, Hunter could see. Purdy learned to accept that small investors had to have a voice and that he should not fight it. He understood that Hunter could be useful—that, although Hunter did not have any control over the small investors, at least they would listen to him.

Meanwhile, Purdy had immense clout with public figures such as Bank of Canada governor Carney and another bright economist, Tiff Macklem, who got involved in the ABCP brief through senior roles at both the Department of Finance and the Bank of Canada. Purdy appreciated the young economist's intelligence, and Macklem watched Purdy perform his quiet magic. "He brought enormous credibility, great respect from all parties, and a reputation for being a fair-minded consensus builder," Macklem would later say. "At the same time, he could be tough: he is an experienced negotiator; he knows how to forge a consensus and knows when to put some pressure on."

In April came the announcement that the retail investors would be paid off in full. Canaccord Genuity put up some money, and it was an open secret that the Caisse de dépôt and at least one major bank had played a big role. On April 25, 96 percent of 1,940 investors approved the restructuring plan at a Toronto meeting. And on June 5, Mr. Justice Campbell approved the plan.

In late June, a group of corporate noteholders took their objections to the Ontario Court of Appeal, but the court agreed that the plan should go ahead. A request to appeal went all the way up to the Supreme Court of Canada. As Purdy waited through the court procedures, markets turned from nervous to nightmarish.

On September 7, 2008 the Crawford committee's first anniversary, the US government took over Freddie Mac and Fannie Mae, the two companies which then owned or guaranteed about half of the United States' $12 trillion mortgage market. Then the cards tumbled. On September 14, the massive investment bank Merrill Lynch was sold to JP Morgan amid fears of a liquidity crisis and collapse. The next day, venerable Lehman Brothers filed for bankruptcy protection. The interest ratios in the ABCP market went crazy, putting the Crawford committee's year of work at peril. It would have to go back to the drawing board with an amended deal.

"After Lehman collapsed, it was so disheartening," Rubenstein recalls. "There was the fallout, spreads widened, and the paper looked more risky again." In fact, the gods had been good to the ABCP crisis managers. Had they chosen Lehman Brothers as their financial advisor, the process would have been further thrown off track by the firm's collapse. And had they floated the new instruments earlier, there would have been massive—and real—calls for collateral, which would have driven the market into another crisis. "Had an agreement been reached more quickly, it would have probably fallen apart the day after Lehman failed," said one person associated with the deal. Sometimes, it is better to be a little late.

Amid the carnage, it was almost overlooked that, on September 19, the Supreme Court of Canada refused to hear arguments challenging the restructuring plan. Legally, the deal was on track; in terms of the market, it was a mess. The rate spreads got uglier, making the original deal less viable. "Macro events around the world just kept conspiring against us," Halperin says, which meant that the committee finally had to seek government help.

It was then that Purdy used his relationships with Flaherty, Carney, and Macklem to try to wring additional collateral guarantees out of the federal and provincial governments. And they came through: Ottawa pitched in, then got Quebec to do so, and Ontario and Alberta also contributed. The standby arrangements guaranteed that there would not be a default for the first eighteen months of the new notes. Fortunately, the guarantees never had to be called, and they expired without governments paying a dime. In fact, the governments made money from fees for providing this backstop.

Still, it was a wrenching concession by the feds. Right from the beginning, they were adamant that these were private sector investments and that there must be a private sector solution—that the federal government was not in the business of bailing out bad investments. But the Lehman-induced volatility had created a gap between the private banks' commitment and the collateral support that was needed. It was in the best interests of Canada if government came in and bridged that gap. That required a standby injection of $1.3 billion from Ottawa, which was a lot of money, but relative to the $32 billion—or $300 billion—at risk, not a huge amount. The three provinces ponied up some more, creating close to $5 billion of additional backup. For these governments, it was an Ed Clark kind of decision—it was not their problem, but if the system failed, it would become their problem. It showed just how dangerous the world had become in the second half of 2008.

Once the federal government agreed to inject some money, it got leverage with the parties—and it was a big part of pushing the process to a solution. Behind the scenes, the Bank of Canada's Mark Carney was playing a more active role in getting the players onside, at one point making a timely call to the Deutsche Bank CEO in Germany, according to a report by the *Globe*'s Boyd Erman. In the background, public authorities worldwide started to get a handle on the crisis. The key was a historic G7 meeting in October, where finance ministers and central bankers put up a plan which said there would not be another Lehman.

By Christmas, the financial press was reporting that the seventeen-month-long nightmare appeared to be near an end. But there were still wrinkles to iron out as Steve Halperin's "interesting little job" extended to another Christmas. The marathon process had killed marriages, wrecked relationships, created family tensions as too many planes were stuck on runways, and too many fathers and mothers were talking on the phone well into Christmas morning. Steve Halperin managed to get away for both his daughters' weddings during the period. Fran Guolo saw her daughter's first birthday come and go. Everyone talked to everyone else about their problems.

Just before Christmas, Guolo was with her family at a chalet in Ontario ski country. She was on the phone with a gaggle of lawyers and Bank of Canada people when she saw her four-year-old son barrelling down the slopes. She blurted into the phone, "Oh, my God. My son is coming down the hill and he is going too fast." Fortunately, her husband got things under control. Everyone on the phone call relaxed—a collective sigh heard round the world.

There were the battles over fees—who paid them, who got them. If you give up your life, your marriage, your health, you had to feel it was all worth it. It was late in the game, tempers got hot. At one point, Purdy snapped out of his calm demeanour and instructed a senior lawyer to tell another team member: "What a baby, tell him to quit whining!" But everyone understood. In the high energy, ego-soaked world of finance, fees were a badge of honour.

In mid-January 2009, Mr. Justice Campbell approved the final version of the restructuring. Not everyone was happy with the outcome. People ended up with notes with no value, no market, only Purdy's promise that "it is expected" there will be a secondary market.

In May, financier Seymour Schulich summed up the frustration in a letter to the editor in the *Financial Post*:

Purdy Crawford must be delusional, in my opinion, if he thinks he got a great deal for the ABCP paper investors.

He spends 18 months and only 10% of these swindled ABCP holders get their money back. This quarter, the banks who gained litigation immunity and his lawyer-colleagues steal $200-million in fees, so there's not a cent available to pay any interest.

The holders of this paper in many cases had funds frozen that had been earmarked for employment-creating capital projects.

Other holders were pension funds. This paper today is no bid.

The remaining 90% of the holders can't get 1¢ on the dollar for this paper that the bankers foisted on unsuspecting short-term paper buyers.

The banks, the government and the judiciary have all played a role in dissipating $30-billion in investor funds with no recourse allowed.

His final statement was most damning: "Mr. Crawford should, in my opinion, retire permanently and stop helping investors."

For corporate treasurers—in the mining industry, particularly—Schulich's letter resonated. They knew where he was coming from. A lot of companies had been damaged by the restructuring because they were given bad advice. Some of the bigger operators made deals with their bankers who had sold them the stuff, but, failing that, they were out millions—unless they could wait. Some couldn't, and they were sacrificed in the interests of saving the system. And, most galling, they couldn't sue.

Schulich's public letter baffled and hurt Purdy because he thought he had a good relationship with the colourful financier. He had got to know him in the 1980s while raising money for McGill University, from which Schulich had graduated. Schulich, a storied investor who had made a fortune in gold mining but owned a swath of interests, had gone on a philanthropic spree, giving away more than $100 million to universities and leaving a trail of faculties with his name on them. He was about to give $20 million to the Dalhousie law school in exchange for putting his name on the school. When his letter scorching Crawford appeared, some law school supporters, loyal to Purdy, felt Dalhousie should walk away from the money—that taking it would show disrespect to the school's greatest graduate. Purdy said, basically, forget it. If you can get Seymour Schulich to fork out $20 million for the law school, take the money. Life is too short. Keep your eye on the horizon, not the small cuts. "I didn't say anything—you can't win those arguments."

Purdy's response during this period was gracious, recalled Seymour Schulich, who, five years after writing his withering letter, had gained a little perspective on the ABCP resolution and its architect. Schulich was not sure whether Crawford could have done anything different under the circumstances and given the realities of Canada. Schulich—never one to shrink from controversy—saw the ABCP restructuring as the product of political and judicial systems that will always tilt toward protecting the banks, while the interests of customers take a back seat. But Purdy, he added, "is not a bad guy."

Some of the ABCP players got together at a deal-closing reception in Toronto, and Andrew Kresse, the kid from Buffalo, was given an honorary Canadian passport. He then went back to New York to work with JP Morgan's client companies on their hedging strategies. Carney, having made his reputation as a cool-headed crisis manager, went to the top job at the Bank of England. Tiff Macklem, passed over for the Bank of Canada governor's job, eventually would leave the post of the Bank's senior deputy governor and become dean of the Rotman School of Management at the University of Toronto.

Jim Flaherty, the finance minister, saw his reputation buffed by the successful restructuring, and his management of the financial crisis enhanced his global stature. But after eight years as finance minister and two decades in political life, he decided in early 2014 to head back into the private sector. As he prepared for the transition, he died of a massive heart attack. Purdy had grown fond of the diminutive finance minister who responded so well to his calls for help. He also appreciated Flaherty's role in Ottawa's financial commitment to expand nationally one of Crawford's projects, the Purdy Crawford Chair in Aboriginal Business at Cape Breton University.

Henri-Paul Rousseau would leave the Caisse de dépôt before the reorganization was complete, his reputation a bit frayed but held together by his role in salvaging the ABCP market. Rousseau took a big job with Power Corporation, the financial conglomerate controlled by the Desmarais family.

Gale Rubenstein and Francesca Guolo went on to other assignments, as did Steve Halperin, although nothing in his career would have such intensity, stress, and society-spanning implications. Goodmans had been lucky to take the lead on two big problem briefs: the failed privatization of telecom giant BCE and the ABCP crisis. Purdy remembers the firm's managing partner thanking him for the ABCP work because it got Goodmans through the recession in good shape. Other law firms might say the same thing.

Brian Hunter got his money back, and with about 4 percent interest—not bad for that period in history. Lots of us would take that. In March 2009, Purdy travelled to Calgary for the annual meeting of Canadian National, of which he was a director emeritus. Hunter smiles at the memory. "He kindly invited me for breakfast at the Palliser Hotel." It was their only extensive one-on-one meeting, and it was low key and pleasant, "just a couple of guys having a chat. It was nice of him to actually bother to take the time."

Hunter, like Purdy, had concluded that "you have to keep the emotion out of it—you're pissed off and you want to lash out and everybody has a need for vengeance, but this wasn't going to happen." He had learned: "Don't tilt at windmills, see what you can get done." Purdy Crawford couldn't have said it better—if you can't get the perfect, go for the possible.

The new notes were trading in the secondary market, and hedge funds started buying them. The values moved steadily up, and some people were making a lot of money. Some investors sold out; others with longer time horizons, like the pension funds, held on. By the winter of 2013–14, valuations on the notes were up to the mid-90-cents level on each dollar invested—not yet a dollar on a dollar but getting close.

Bea Crawford got Purdy back. They thought it was going to be a shorter assignment, and as it dragged on, it concerned Bea. But after sixty years of marriage, she knew this kind of job was Purdy's very essence. And it turned out well. "It would have been devastating if it had not been so good in how it turned out," Bea remarks.

It was widely agreed that he had achieved a lot—first in unlocking more than $32 billion in stranded assets and then getting it done within eighteen months. "The money he saved investors is easily $10 to $20 billion, and his salary of $40,000 a month is nothing," says one banker close to the scene. Goodmans, the law firm, paid tribute to him by establishing the Purdy Crawford Fund for Global Financial Markets, a $500,000 initiative at Dalhousie's Schulich School of Law for supporting scholarly work on financial regulation, risk, innovation, and ethics. Goodmans put in $100,000, with the rest coming from firms that had a lot of reason to honour Purdy Crawford: Bank of Nova Scotia, Royal Bank, Canaccord, three credit union centrals, Desjardins, JP Morgan Canada, TD, and Osler.

The plaudits poured in. Now in London, Mark Carney was unstinting in his praise:

> Purdy Crawford is a quite simply a Canadian institution. His rich and varied contributions to Canada's business and legal communities, and our national financial system, speak for themselves. In particular, his tireless leadership, dedication and creativity during the non-bank ABCP crisis were core ingredients to its successful resolution.
>
> I can say with conviction that we would not have crossed the finish line were it not for Purdy. Many Canadians, including thousands of retail investors who were made whole on the deal, owe Purdy a debt of gratitude for being the driving force in all aspects of the workout, from the initial standstill agreement, to the eventual re-floating of the longer-term notes, and the much higher

returns investors are facing today. It took a unique Canadian to bring to life a uniquely Canadian solution to what could have been a devastating slip over the precipice of the global financial crisis.

Ed Clark announced his impending retirement and looked back on the stormy period when Carney and Crawford were urging him to chip in with some money. Since then, the Great Recession had set in and battered the US and European economies. In Canada, the effects were less painful, and TD was positioned to pick up more assets south of the border in making its big bet on North American retail customers, using the same consumer-focused strategy that Canada Trust had developed in the 1970s and 1980s.

TD benefited from Canada's relative strength through the crisis—and once again Purdy was the guy standing beside Clark in a knife fight. A country needs "moral authority leaders" like Crawford, and there are fewer and fewer of those people, Clark says. "Countries need those kinds of people to call other people in and say 'let's do this—leave your personal interests at the door'."

A failed ABCP would have meant higher costs of capital and much lower confidence in Canada's banks, corporations, and institutions. It would have made Ed Clark's job, and his expansion vision, much harder—and the same could be said of other financial industry players. During the market meltdown, Clark observes, it would have been a total shame for Canada "if, in so many ways, we got it right and in this one place we got it wrong." He adds that "we could have ended up in the same result as people who got it wrong in multiple ways."

It could be said, he maintains, that "Purdy saved us from that."

Chapter Thirteen

# CHIEF RISING TIDE

J oe Shannon had a problem. The Nova Scotia entrepreneur was about to witness a milestone in the development of Cape Breton University, the hometown school that Shannon had backed with money and energy for twenty-five years. It was the day that Purdy Crawford, who was championing Aboriginal education, would be made an honorary chief of the Membertou First Nation, an enterprising Mi'kmaq community not far from downtown Sydney. As was customary with such events, Crawford needed a title—and not just Chief Crawford. But Shannon and Membertou Chief Terry Paul had failed to come up with something evocative of Purdy's contributions.

The day of the ceremony—June 24, 2010—Shannon was still grappling with a name while driving from his home along the western edge of Cape Breton Island toward Sydney. "I was thinking up and down the road, and boiled it down to two names," Shannon recalls. Maybe Purdy could be Chief Five Islands, named for the Nova Scotia community of his birth. But, in truth, Purdy was not a guy who builds islands—he builds bridges—and so that was scrapped. The other thought was that the Bay of Fundy produces the highest tides in the world. So why not call him Chief Rising Tide? As the saying goes, "a rising tide lifts all boats."

"That is really the character of Purdy Crawford—he will jump into difficult situations," Shannon mused. And now he was working with the university to lift Aboriginal people and had given his name and financial support to the Purdy Crawford Chair in Aboriginal Business, aimed at promoting the participation of Aboriginal youth in post-secondary business education.

The high point of the ceremony was when Chief Paul bestowed a spectacular headdress on Purdy Crawford, now Chief Rising Tide.

Purdy has certainly adhered to that principle. He is all about lifting boats, and Shannon is the model of the vessel Purdy likes to lift. Shannon came out of grade ten as a dump-truck driver, then started to build a trucking business of his own. His company is now reputedly the largest highway trucker of petroleum products in the country. Forget about buried pipelines—Joe Shannon has a pipeline of trucks always moving across the country. He has taken his energy into all kind of businesses, including real estate, self-storage, and a chain of retirement homes that are among the favourite destinations for elderly Maritimers.

In his early seventies, he now wants to back education in Cape Breton because, he feels, the economic game has changed dramatically. If Cape Breton is to thrive, its young people need to find opportunity at home, instead of moving to central or western Canada. And it needs private business, not the old government corporations of the past. In any case, government was giving up on supporting jobs through giveaways. But the region needed a good business school, and so Joe Shannon developed his dream for a stronger business faculty at Cape Breton University.

He shared that dream with a guy he met on an airplane, a fellow named Purdy Crawford. They got to talking a lot about their backgrounds. "Most people are nosy, but Purdy is just curious," Shannon notes. "You don't mind talking to a guy who is curious if that's sincere." And Joe Shannon's businesses and his passion for Cape

Breton University are the kinds of things that engage Purdy Crawford. His heart is still with Mount Allison University, and that is the focus of much of the Crawford family's volunteerism. But he is a sucker for all kinds of educational projects that help lift boats and decided to back Joe Shannon as an advisory board member for what is now Cape Breton University's Shannon School of Business. Joe meets Purdy's first requirements for a good leader: he is smart, and he has passion. He has the "fire in the belly" that Purdy saw in another upwardly mobile Cape Bretoner, Annette Verschuren. That fire lies at the heart of Crawford's leadership recipe.

There is a lot of talk today about what makes leaders. Leadership is one of the hottest topics in management journals and business school curricula. The role models held up for emulation are high-profile executives in public or private life—Steve Jobs, Richard Branson, Jack Welch—often polarizing figures with a gift for thrusting themselves into the public eye. Purdy presents an alternative model of character-centred, emotionally grounded leadership that is just as effective and more enduring. But the one thing all the great leaders share is passion.

Other ingredients also make up the Crawford recipe of leadership traits:

- Be interested in people, including in their lives beyond their work and profession. Who are their partners and children? What drives their goals and hopes and fears?
- Read widely and deeply. Purdy has always believed great leaders are not narrowly tied to their disciplines but know about the world, public policy, and social issues.
- Take time to think about a hard decision. Good choices come from sleeping on them, contemplating them, and coming at them fresh.
- Look for input outside familiar circles. Purdy's career is a model on this theme: he is a man's man, perhaps, but is comfortable

taking guidance from women. And he is willing to stride out into a buzz saw of criticism if it means getting at the truth.

- Your influence does not come from who you know but who you help along the way. You might not expect a reward, but it is often there—perhaps in the success story of an underdog who comes out of nowhere and exceeds expectations.

- Great networks are not one-dimensional but intersecting arcs of friendship and duty, work, and volunteerism.

- Don't sweat the small stuff. Shrug off small defeats, insults, slights, and imperfections. There is a final goal, and you should keep it in mind and work toward it.

- A blind search for perfection is the enemy of getting things done. Don't look for the perfect solution—look for the one that can succeed, helping the most people. Practise the art of the possible.

- Be bold in your career and your investments, especially at a young age, when you can suffer a setback, learn from it, and move on.

- See the big picture, and don't get caught in "the dailyness of life."

- Don't forget the people who got you there—the hometown folks, the family members, the parents and teachers, and, yes, especially the mentors.

That final rule is a constant in Purdy Crawford's life. Flash forward to spring 2013. He is attending a gala dinner as Joe Shannon is being inducted into the Canadian Business Hall of Fame. It is Shannon's celebration, but it is also Purdy Crawford's night. Purdy worked hard to get Shannon into the hall, because it meant recognition for an entrepreneur whose name was unfamiliar to central Canadians and who came from an overlooked part of the country. The audience of more than a thousand includes a large contingent of men and women, from coast to coast, who have assumed top leadership roles because of a connection, a tip, an idea gleaned from Purdy Crawford. They are all around the room, from Shannon to Annette Verschuren, John Bragg, and Robert Campbell—even Peter Mansbridge, who is hosting the induction ceremony (and who got involved with the Hall of Fame and its sponsor organization, Junior Achievement, at Purdy's urging). They are Purdy's People, a not-so-silent force in our country's business and public life. His impact on corporate governance and securities law has been huge, but it is his mentoring that is his most enduring legacy.

It is actually Crawford's second public event in twenty-four hours. The previous day, he found himself in First Canadian Place, the Toronto office tower that houses the Osler law firm and the headquarters of Bank of Montreal. In a very Bay Street reception room, Purdy was part of what was billed as an old-fashioned ceilidh to honour Shannon and his work at Cape Breton University. The room filled up with the music of the Barra MacNeils, a Cape Breton Celtic group, a smattering of Bay Street luminaries, and a quorum of East Coast types—a few Sobeys, a McCain or two, and lots of Crawfords and Shannons. Joe Shannon himself was a mix of pride and shyness as he steeled himself for all the hoopla around his induction.

Purdy was using a wheelchair—he had slowed down physically and his pulmonary problems had worsened since the ABCP crisis, but he was still engaged. Called forward to speak, he stepped gingerly to the mic and made a speech about Joe Shannon's great achievement. Suddenly, the eyes sparkled, the big, friendly smile lit up the room, and, as if to capture the spirit of the occasion, he burst into a rendition of one of his favourite songs: *Got my dancing shoes on, got my Sunday best...* It was the signature tune of Charlie Chamberlain and Marg Osburne, the two singers who fronted the popular Maritimes fiddle band, Don Messer and His Islanders, on their 1950s and '60s TV show. For a moment, Purdy was transported back to the church basements and community halls of his youth. Despite the four homes, the big portfolio, the honorary degrees, he was still essentially the boy from Five Islands. Emotionally, he was back in the living room of the old farmhouse that used to be part of Bea's family, where he could sit with his books, his family photos, and his children and grandchildren, and it was like he never left home.

~

Purdy Crawford died on August 12, 2014, at age eighty-two, just as this book was in the final stages of production. Bea was by his side, as she had been for sixty-three years.

# ACKNOWLEDGEMENTS

S everal years ago, John Bragg suggested an idea for my next book, a biography of his friend Purdy Crawford. John saw it as a story of Purdy's large influence on Canadian leaders and a tribute to his extraordinary mentoring. We took the idea to Robert Campbell, president of Mount Allison University, which had been so crucial in nurturing the young Purdy Crawford—and which Purdy, as an adult, has been so passionate in supporting. Mount Allison has been the indispensable sponsor of this book—and I benefited greatly from the support and feedback of Robert and of Gloria Jollymore, the vice-president of university advancement. And John Bragg has remained an unwavering ally.

Purdy bought in to the project, although he was a little abashed at the idea of a biography written about him. He devoted many hours to conversation with me, even when he did not feel all that well. It became more than a job, but a friendship that I value immensely. And I talked to many people whose lives Purdy Crawford has touched. This is a large community, and I regret I could not talk to each of them. I extend thanks to the following who did share their thoughts: Deborah Alexander, David Allgood, Howard Beck, John Bragg, Scott Brison, John Buchanan, Mark Carney, Tullio Cedraschi, Ed Clark, Brian Lee Crowley, Peter Dey, Sean Foran, Martin Friedland,

Harvey Gilmour, Constance Glube, James Gray, Francesca Guolo, Steve Halperin, Hunter Harrison, Brian Hunter, Chris Huskilson, Maureen Jensen, David Johnston, Tim Kennish, Brian Levitt, Bob Lindsay, Jim Lisson, Lynn Loewen, Ed Lumley, Sue Lucas, Tiff Macklem, Peter Mansbridge, Joe Martin, Margaret McCain, Michael McCain, Scott McCain, Frank McKenna, Nancy McKinstry, David McLean, John McLennan, Ian Newbould, Saul Paton, Jack Petch, Dale Ponder, Gale Rubenstein, Dawn Russell, Seymour Schulich, Joe Shannon, Rob Prichard, Janet Salter, Paul Tellier, David Sobey, Donald Sobey, Frank Thomas, Annette Verschuren, George Vesely, Benita Warmbold, Susan Wolburgh Jenah, and Torrance Wylie. And thanks, too, to the occasional contributor who preferred not to be named in the book.

This biography could not have been written without Purdy's warm and welcoming wife Bea and the couple's helpful, enthusiastic children: Barbara Crawford, David Crawford, Heather Crawford, Mary Crawford, Sarah Crawford, and Suzanne Crawford. Thanks to Bea's brother Steve Corbett for giving me a tour of Purdy's world in Five Islands, Nova Scotia.

Boyd Erman, my former colleague at the *Globe and Mail*, generously read the key ABCP chapters. The *Globe* and the *National Post* filled in key parts of Purdy's life. Marnie McLean at Osler was very helpful, as was Jill Vardy, communications chief at the Bank of Canada. Barry Critchley provided a timely assist. Many others also contributed—at Mount Allison, at Osler, and in all the places where Purdy's impact is felt.

I am grateful to Nimbus Publishing of Halifax and its managing editor Patrick Murphy for taking on this project and being so supportive in all its phases. Thanks, as well, to Barry Norris for his alert and informed editing. My agent Dean Cooke is a rock for me. My wife Elaine is the valuable first reader of my books and leads me through the peaks and valleys. Daughters Katie and Martha, son-in-law Thomas, and my wonderful granddaughter Ellie remind me of what is important. My mother, Reta Pitts, my fiercest critic and most loyal reader, asked why this guy Purdy Crawford merited a biography. She did not live long enough to read the answer, but I know she would have loved knowing about Purdy.

# INDEX

## A

Acadia University 132, 140
Adams Committee 55
Adams report 56
A. E. Ames 30
Alexander, Deborah 42–43, 45, 48–52, 56, 88, 111
Allgood, David 45
Allison, Charles Frederick 141
Allstream 103, 164. *See also* AT&T; AT&T Canada
*American Lawyer* v
American Revolution 11, 19
Anti-Inflation Board 52, 82
Armstrong, Christopher 38
Arthur Andersen 104
asset-backed commercial paper (ABCP) 2, 6, 53, 155, 157–59, 161, 163–65, 168–74, 176–77, 179, 181–83
ATB Financial 159
Atlantic Institute for Market Studies (AIMS) 134–35
AT&T 101–02. *See also* Allstream
AT&T Canada 53, 91, 101–04, 161. *See also* Allstream

## B

Baillie, Charles 87
Baillie, Jim 47, 88
Bank of Canada 2, 159, 164, 167, 176, 178–79, 181
Bank of England 181
Bank of Montreal (BMO) 29, 44, 77, 86, 96, 108, 121, 149, 189
Bank of Nova Scotia 42, 57, 93, 183
Barrick Gold 170
BAT Industries 62, 68, 78, 85–86
Bay Street 1, 5, 15, 21–22, 24–26, 30, 32, 35, 37, 40–41, 54, 93, 114, 125, 155–56
BCE 132, 182
Bear Stearns 167
Beattie, Allan 28–30, 33, 44, 46, 112

Beaudoin, Laurent 97
Beck, Howard 37, 40
Bell Canada 93, 101–02
Berkshire Hathaway 151–52
Bethlehem Steel 34–35
Bill of Rights 21
BlackBerry 30, 162
Blake, Cassels 25, 48, 52
Bloom, David 66, 68
BNSF 96–97
Boland, Greg 129–31
Bombardier 97–98
Bombardier, Joseph-Armand 97
Bragg family 5, 104, 132, 144–45
Bragg, John 112, 121, 125, 131–33, 135, 142, 144–46, 152, 189
Bramalea 33, 164
Bray, Harry 38, 49
Brison, Scott 15, 116–17
British Telecom 104
Brock, Bill 86
Broughton, Martin 85–86
Buchanan, John "Hunk" 16–18
Buffett, Warren 132, 151–53
Burns, Nesbitt 96, 108

## C

Caisse de dépôt et placement du Québec 1, 71, 159–60, 169, 176, 181
Campbell, Justice Colin 169, 176, 179
Campbell, Robert 145–47, 189
Canaccord Genuity 171, 173, 176, 183
Canada Development Investment Corporation 75
Canada Northwest Energy Ltd 65
Canada Pension Plan Investment Board 165
Canada Permanent 71
Canada Safeway 136, 138
Canada Trust 5, 69–72, 83–84, 86–88, 137, 184. *See also* CT Financial